SIGNATURE STYLE

TRADITIONAL HOME® BOOKS
DES MOINES, IOWA

MEREDITH® BOOKS

TRADITIONAL HOME®
SIGNATURE
STYLE

Editor: Linda Hallam

Senior Associate Design Director: Richard Michels

Photograper: Gordon Beal

Contributing Editors: Estelle Bond Guralnick, Carla Howard, Nancy Ingram, Heather Lobdell, Bonnie Maharam, Sally Mauer, Hilary Rose

Copy Chief: Catherine Hamrick

Copy and Production Editor: Terri Fredrickson

Contributing Copy Editor: Jennifer Miller

Contributing Proofreaders: Sheila Mauck, May Pas, Debra Morris Smith

Electronic Production Coordinator: Paula Forest

Editorial and Design Assistants: Kaye Chabot, Mary Lee Gavin, Karen Schirm

Production Director: Douglas M. Johnston

Production Manager: Pam Kvitne

Assistant Prepress Manager: Marjorie J. Schenkelberg

MEREDITH® BOOKS

Editor in Chief: James D. Blume

Design Director: Matt Strelecki

Managing Editor: Gregory H. Kayko

Executive Shelter Editor: Denise L. Caringer

Director, Sales & Marketing, Retail: Michael A. Peterson

Director, Sales & Marketing, Special Markets: Rita McMullen

Director, Sales & Marketing, Home & Garden Center Channel: Ray Wolf

Director, Operations: George A. Susral

Vice President, General Manager: Jamie L. Martin

TRADITIONAL HOME® MAGAZINE

Editor in Chief: Karol DeWulf Nickell

Art Director: Jim Darilek

Interior Design Senior Editor: Mitchell Owens

Interior Design Editor: Pamela J. Wilson

MEREDITH PUBLISHING GROUP

President, Publishing Group: Christopher M. Little

Vice President, Consumer Marketing & Development: Hal Oringer

MEREDITH CORPORATION

Chairman and Chief Executive Officer: William T. Kerr

Chairman of the Executive Committee: E. T. Meredith III

All of us at Meredith® Books are dedicated to providing you with information and ideas to enhance your home. We welcome your comments and suggestions. Write to us at: Meredith® Books, Shelter Editorial Department, 1716 Locust St., Des Moines, IA 50309-3023.

If you would like to purchase additional copies of any our books, please check wherever quality books are sold.

Cover Photograph: Gordon Beall. The room shown is on page 59.

CONTENTS

SIGNATURE STYLE
FINDING YOURS

–Karol DeWulf Nickell, Editor In Chief, Traditional Home®

You know it when it finally happens. • Paging

through fashion magazines is still fun, but you

no longer search for the next new thing to try.

Instead, you look for the right dress or suit for you. • You know

what looks good on you. A certain cut, a becoming color...the right

length and a flattering neckline. • You've found your style, and it

feels great. • Now, can you say the same thing about your interiors?

• Why is it a woman (or a man) who has no problem choosing a

stylish and appropriate wardrobe (as well as the right car, the

right wine, and the right vacation spot) often has nightmares

about selecting a wall color? • Perhaps the answer is in this book.

What room pictured *above* would you most like to spend time in? If the answer comes easily, then you know what appeals, and you're well on the way to finding your own signature style. Each room was created by a designer featured in this book and started with an individual affinity that blossomed gracefully into a complete decorating scheme.

When color and pattern are played down, furniture choices become even more important in a room scheme. These five white-on-white rooms by our selected designers illustrate how various styles of furnishings evoke various moods. While contrasting the serious with the just-for-fun can work, it's easier to mix furniture with similar dispositions.

Creating beautiful interiors is as much a personal journey as it is about understanding the color wheel or knowing the difference between cabriole and cartouche. Even if one has the benefit of a formal design education, finding one's own approach to design is an active endeavor. And one worth pursuing as it will forever enhance your enjoyment of life.

Signature Style is all about the many different and fascinating choices we have when it comes to creating our interiors. It explores eight different visions of beauty as seen through the eyes of eight different interior designers from all across the country. These masters of interior design were chosen by the editors of *Traditional Home®* because we admire their work and their personal philosophies that direct them. By dedicating a chapter to each designer and their rooms, we

hope to give you an intimate understanding of how each of these professionals came to their design approaches. We think you'll find that each followed a unique path. And, therein lies the heart of the matter. Some years ago when I had a small design business, I was amazed to find how often the most hesitant client transformed into the most engaged one. One particular case was a husband who initially only wanted to see beiges and neutrals. Four rooms and dozens of hours later, it was at his urging that we selected a regal peacock-feather palette for the couple's

formal dining room. This fortunate phenomenon can be likened to tasting a delectable, exotic dessert for the first time: after discovering it one never hesitates to enjoy it again. The fun of creating beauty that's personal and lasting heightens with each experience.

For most of us, the journey has already begun. We're well past trends and coordinating sets of anything. Our interiors reflect a certain sophistication. Now we just need some help on pulling it all together, or we seek the fresh eye and wise expert who can make our interiors truly special.

But if you're like me, you need a bit of encouragement to get past contemplating the options. So, here are my favorite decorating wisdoms to get you going. I've collected these truisms over the years from the many design sages we've feature in *Traditional Home®:* their simple relevancy never ceases to assist.

Find things you love and build around them. Designers will be the first to tell you that they'd rather not start from scratch. Their best work is a combination of what you love and what they know. Whether you choose to work with an interior designer or not, your starting point need not be an obvious one. While fine art, furnishings, and rugs provide excellent jumping off points for an interior, less stately objects such as collected china or glassware, or a new fabric or wallpaper can also inspire. Try to identify what about the object pleases you—the color, the shape, the era or the style it reflects, and so on. Then build on those characteristics, repeating or contrasting them in your interiors.

Look first, read second, buy third. With so many choices and influences, the pleasure of "trying things on" without committing to them is also a prudent practice. As a magazine editor and decorating enthusiast, I strongly recommend a constant diet of interior design magazines as a way to see all kinds of design solutions, products, colors, and styles without dipping into your furnishings budget. I also advise you to clip or mark the rooms you like best as a way to develop a personal design library you can reference through the years. Paging through a folder of collected photos will quickly reveal what kinds of things continually

catch your eye. It's important to educate yourself about the objects of design. Knowing a Goddard-style block-front desk by sight is fine, but knowing that an original block-front desk and bookcase attributed to John Goddard sold for more than $12 million in 1989 makes owning a modern-day adaptation better. When you sign the sizable check for the desk, your head and your heart will be aligned.

Do it with someone. While this isn't essential, decorating with someone, either a friend or a professional interior designer, can be more fun and oftentimes more rewarding. Select someone whose eye you trust and with whom you can be perfectly frank. While compromise is often a good thing in a personal relationship, you don't want to feel as though you compromised when it comes to your sofa.

A favorite decorating adage is "Knowing the rules allows you to break them." Such freedom from the expected results in charming touches such as an Oriental figure mischieviously placed just outside a formal dining room, **opposite**, and the inspired use of a formerly formal dining room as a theatrical mirrored music room, **above**.

Frank Lloyd Wright said: "God is in the details," and all the designers in this book would agree. Whether it's applied detail, such as passementerie trimming a tablecloth, **top right**, or a painted motif on a chair, **bottom left**, or the collective impact of carefully chosen accessories, **top left**, **bottom right**, and **opposite**, details complete your interior.

Choosing to work with a professional interior designer can be the best investment you make when it comes to reaching your design goals on time and on budget. But you need to shop around for the right match. And you need to be honest about what you want, and how much time and money you're willing to commit. Again, design books and magazines are excellent sources for interior designers. For an introduction to designers in your area, attend decorator showhouses where you can meet and talk with a number of designers during one tour.

Edit. Add. Refresh. While some design titans of the past might argue, today's approach to rooms is that they're not works of art, done to perfection and forever frozen in time. A room is never "done;" it is a continuum. While the basic furnishings might remain for years, their coverings and arrangement might change to accommodate changing needs and wants. Take a look at the rooms in this book. While each is a complete vision, it isn't an inflexible one. Elements can and will be changed as time goes by.

Knowing the rules allows you to break them—beautifully. This is probably designers' all-time favorite adage. What it means is that if you take the time to learn the basics then they become your tools for innovation. For instance, once you can recognize classic proportions in architecture, furniture design, and window treatments, you can use an underscaled or overscaled element to create interest and impact. The same certainly pertains to all the other rules about combining decorative arts styles and eras. A Queen Anne-style table is perfectly paired with 18th-century early Georgian chairs, but why not try a synergistic marriage with Eames chairs from the 1940s?

Follow your instincts. If you love purple, try it in one of your rooms. If you've always been drawn to French toiles, do a whole wonderful room covered in them.

It's never too late. Two professional designers featured in this book found design as a second career. If it took these pros that long to find their true passion, your interest as a decorating enthusiast is encouraged, whenever and however.

•

Signature Style is a celebration of interior design done to please the individual, but it was created by a collaboration of many. It has been a pleasure—and a personal journey—to work with many fine professionals whose outstanding talents, insights, and efforts combined to make this a milestone book. My special thanks to Linda Hallam, Rich Michels, and Gordon Beall. To our eight featured interior designers whose magnificent rooms literally made my heart leap as we laid them out on the pages and whose words combine genius, humor, and common sense, bravo! You never fail to inspire me.

TRANSCONTI

FRENCH

STYLE

WITH CHARLES

The ageless appeal of French-style furnishings

isn't difficult to understand. Designed to

Charles Faudree

both flatter and function, they exude a

warmth and "joy of life" that are universally admired.

NENTAL

But how does one integrate these

wonderful pieces into interiors for the 21st century?

This is a lesson learned superbly from

the recognized master, Charles Faudree.

FAUDREE

From the high styles of the 18th and 19th centuries to the present, the French have influenced American architecture and interior design. Our grand homes and, later, glittering city apartments have reflected the influences of the European country most closely associated with the decorative arts and graces. As interest in French decorating and decorative arts has grown, Americans have discovered provincial furniture and arts—the less formal styles and

"COUNTRY FRENCH PIECES LEND THEMSELVES TO AN ARTFUL MIXING."

unpolished woods of the French countryside. Country French combines the rustic with touches of the refined in a style that's livable in its casual, understated elegance. The style welcomes each acquisition, melding periods and provinces with warmth, ease, and graciousness.

With his own French ancestry, Tulsa, Oklahoma, designer Charles Faudree works in a milieu inspired by his love of all things French. Yet at the same time, his interiors are a unique, artful mix of prints and patterns with both country and high-style furniture. Rather than strictly replicating historic French styles of decorating, the designer is known as the master of pairing Gallic architectural detailing and furnishings with charming English art and accessories. This signature look, with more color, pattern, and accessories than strictly French decorating, creates a lively,

To balance the painting above the painted 1820 French buffet, Faudree arranged blue-and-white porcelains and stacked an octagonal Louis XVI (1780) barometer. The polychrome altar sticks, converted into lamps, bridge the divergent heights.

The barn-wood walls pair with refined pieces, such as the 18th-century fruitwood clock, English majolica stick stand, and Victorian tole coal stove. Brackets decorate walls as they elevate Staffordshire and blue-and-white porcelains. **Opposite:** The Louis XVI chair displays an unusual and highly collectible majolica hat-shape cheese dome.

"I MIGHT WRAP A NEW LINEN FABRIC ON AN
ANCIENT CHAIR WITH FLAKING PAINT."

L'AGE D'OR DU SIÈGE PAILLÉ

THE HOUSE & GARDEN BOOK OF
COUNTRY ROOMS   LEONIE HIGHTON   VENDOME

EDITIONS CÔTE SUD S.A.
SECRETS OF PROVENCE

MUSTIQUE   ARNE HASSELQVIST & ALFRED SCHWEITZMAN

pretty style that has warmed homes for more than 20 years, and has incorporated porcelains and art from across Europe.

Despite an early passion for France and England and a stint at the Kansas City Art Institute, Faudree collected and decorated only for himself until he was 38. "I realized I was doing nothing creative with my life," he says. "I moved back to Oklahoma and redid my sister's house."

From the beginning of his design career, Faudree worked with the light woods and carved detailing of Country French pieces. "They are not so decorated with ormolu or gilt as is some traditional French furniture," he explains. "There is a simplicity, a gentle softness to the furnishings that I find very calming, soothing. The French favor pine and fruitwood, while most English furniture is characterized by dark woods, such as mahogany. And the Country French pieces, which aren't highly polished, lend themselves more to an artful mixing of fabrics, colors, and textures than do pieces in the English Country style."

Such carved or painted provincial pieces, along with armoires and a grand mix of chairs, enliven the homes Faudree decorates. Light-wood French antiques dominate, with pieces displaying undulating, carved arabesques and floral garlands. "I love the carving on the pieces; it gives movement to the furniture," the designer says.

He appreciates pine furniture, often painted in light tints and brighter colors, for accents. "Because the French have

Left: In the Gallic design of symmetrical arrangements, English Adam-style elbow chairs flank the early-18th-century bow-front commode from Southwestern France. Ebony and gilt brackets are in the Louis XVI style. **Opposite top:** The graceful 19th-century walnut bergère is in the Louis XVI style. **Opposite bottom:** The rare 19th-century bust depicts a blackamoor market vendor.

21

a long, hot, dry summer season, their furnishings made of pine would traditionally have been painted to protect them from the sun," Faudree explains. "That's why so much 18th-century furniture has survived." Today, the sun-faded colors, valued for their patina of age and distressed finishes, add character and relax interiors of even formal rooms.

As a creator of warm, personal spaces where comfort reigns, the designer has no qualms about mixing furniture from different provinces and combining fine antiques with 19th- and early-20th-century reproductions. Likewise, he takes license with accessories and art, incorporating both high-style gilded French mirrors and ormolu accessories as well as some very English pieces into the rich mix. "I love English paintings in French frames; the contrast between the rather restrained quality of the English style and the more ornate, voluptuous French style is very wonderful to me.," Faudree says. The subject matter of English art—landscapes and animals, particularly dogs—appeals to the designer. So, too, do British ceramics. He imports Staffordshire figures, transfer ware, and hand-painted crockery. The designer also collects, for himself and for clients, the blue-and-white export porcelains, originally made in China for the European market, and needlepoint from the British Isles, which he

frames for art or makes into his signature, lushly over-stuffed and lavishly trimmed accent pillows.

In his groupings, Faudree arranges with symmetry, imposing order on often disparate decorative arts. "I gravitate to orderly, symmetrical arrangements with a focal point, which is actually quite French," he says. By imposing order with the use of balanced arrangements, the designer says he can indulge in his love of beautiful objects without cluttering or overpowering even small sitting rooms.

And equally integral to Faudree's style is the melding of antique furniture and decorative arts into their settings. "I enjoy the richness of French pieces and English art with the backgrounds and materials of French houses," he says. This means introducing key elements, such as beams on the ceiling, wood paneling on the walls, and tile floors into the houses he helps clients build or remodel. The warmth of these backgrounds creates the kinds of gracious and comfortable spaces that easily welcome the collections and personal family mementos so illustrative of his always inviting yet dressy style.

When possible, he works salvaged French mantels and other architectural fragments into these backgrounds. "It's hard to think of a French house where the hearth isn't important," he says. "There is a beauty to the wood and

Opposite: The open kitchen shelves allow the utilitarian and the beautiful to meld as a charming domestic still life. The carved cows are 19th-century Swiss and Tyrolean. The glazed terra-cotta Italian urn is one of Faudree's favorite Paris flea-market finds. **Left:** Light matte-finished and distressed woods with carved detailing immediately set a Country French mood in this decorative kitchen. Casement windows, curved iron pulls, stone countertops, and the bull's-head bracket allude to Provençal kitchens. A rare German lusterware hot wine pot, circa 1860, graces the window. **Above left:** Collections, here blue-and-white export porcelains in an aged cupboard, enliven Faudree's beautifully decorated interiors. The early-19th-century jardiniere on the floor is enamel on iron. **Above right:** A child's wheelbarrow recalls the pastoral touches that have graced French designs since the late 18th century.

the carving of antique mantels that I find very appealing." Even when a room has a fine mantel, the designer follows his own rule of choosing a major furniture piece that anchors the scheme. "Just one serious piece of furniture—such as an armoire or a chest—will make the rest of it seem important."

For clients who are beginning to collect, Faudree says he advocates purchasing such major investment pieces for each main room of their home. Not only

"I ALWAYS START WITH A PIVOTAL MATERIAL AS THE MAJOR SOURCE OF COLOR AND PATTERN."

does such a piece make a decorating statement, but it will be used for years, often in home after home, he says. But using all serious pieces in a room isn't how Faudree likes to decorate. "I may place an elegant piece of furniture next to a primitive one, or wrap a new linen fabric on an ancient chair with flaking paint or worn carving. Those are the kinds of juxtapositions I like best. They give all the pieces more life. The mix of favorite pieces is the fun of decorating."

An antique Italian chandelier and old French doors graciously age a dining room with Directoire-style chairs. Pug dogs are German porcelain. The centerpiece tole jardiniere is French Restoration, circa 1820. **Opposite:** Faudree combines two favorites in red-and-white toile and blue-and-white porcelains.

In a cozy library sitting room, a Chinese tea tin groups with a French café table, perfect for books and collectibles, and provincial-style wing chairs. The lamp was crafted from a Staffordshire figurine.

Above: Creating a cozy mix, a French bronze of a Cavalier King Charles spaniel finds a home under the painted Régence-style beech-wood table with a rare fabric top. The painting is 19th-century Scottish. Near right: Pillows are crafted from a Victorian beadwork tea cozy, circa 1860. Far right: Faudree elevates favorite Staffordshire pieces for impact.

29

The same juxtaposition of a major design element with supporting players creates Faudree's well-known lush color and pattern schemes in his own style rather than the French tradition. While the French use fabric patterns sparingly, often displaying only one or two in a room, Faudree loves a sumptuous bouquet of patterns and textures, old favorites mixed with the newest fabric-house designs. In this, he takes his cue from the English, who mix patterns and fabrics in their country houses.

"I've always started with a pivotal material as a major source of color and pattern," the designer says. "It may be a rich velvet or a playful cotton, a print or a plaid. And I'm always inspired by new fabric patterns. That's what keeps this style of decorating fresh. The clear colors of new fabrics breathe life into antiques."

But of all the fabrics Faudree enjoys, toile de Jouy, the always-classic French-style print, is most closely associated with his work. He gravitates to the scenic, pastoral designs favored for the original toiles, but he also chooses the simpler florals or even unusual animal-print toiles. In his mixes, the designer often pairs a cotton or linen toile fabric with a matching wallpaper, and he employs both in broad strokes. "Usually, I start with toile for the draperies or on the walls or both," he says. "And then I add it for chair upholstery, pillows, and chair seats. It's truly the one fabric I always love and never tire of. I was delighted to find a wine-red and putty toile that I used in my bedroom and bath. Red is my favorite color, so I always have at least one red room in every house I decorate.

Although color is subjective, Faudree says he finds that red, in paint or wallpaper, is the one color that gives instant impact to a room of any size. For him, the passionate shade is particularly inviting in personal spaces, such as small sitting rooms or bedrooms. Along with the red, Faudree arranges blue-and-white porcelains, which he has collected since college, with painted tole accents in antique metal light fixtures, lamps, and decorative, antique cachepots.

Faudree-designed rooms are comfortable, inviting retreats despite the fine pedigrees of many of the major pieces and art. "I say I never know where to stop, but I do edit," he adds. "I try to create what is pleasing to the eye. I can't narrow things down. There's far too much in life that interests me. My philosophy has always been, 'Too much is never enough.' I know my houses are overfurnished, overdecorated, and overaccessorized. What I do contradicts all rules of design perspective, but the more you get in a room, the bigger it will look. And I wouldn't have it any other way."

Opposite: The French oak sideboard from Picardy, with a distinctive open center, displays an English Victorian transfer ware footbath, circa 1840, and lamps crafted from antique French bronze fire dogs. For a lively twist, an unusual Chinese-motif leopard toile covers the chairs. **Above:** The dining room's Welsh dresser is George III English oak.

Lamps made from figures of English military heroes flank the reproduction tole bed. Framed English needlepoint is circa 1850. The circa Louis XV commode is from the Ile de France. Because of their two-color schemes, toiles, such as this wine-and-putty linen, are effective backdrops for art.

Opposite: Faudree balances the Louis XVI-style walnut bergère wing chair with the William IV-style English library table, which displays a lamp converted from a Napoleon III candlestick, circa 1870. The stool is a Louis XV taboret, circa 1760. Above: In a luxurious master bath with wine-and-putty toile wallpaper, the Charles X ebony-and-gilt mirror hangs over a 19th-century cherry buffet from Burgundy, transformed into a vanity. The small table is a French mahogany rafraîchissoir (servante). Above right: A Louis XVI-style painted Duchese bergère groups with a Louis XV six-leg taboret, circa 1760, in the master bath. The Régence bleached oak bibliothèque, circa 1730, enriches the library look. Right: In an antiques-filled powder room, French oil burners, converted into sconces, and floral prints flank a 19th-century Louis XVI-style gilt mirror. The figure is an antique Portuguese mannequin.

A lover of animals—especially dogs—and of European history, Charles Faudree collects antique English Staffordshire figures, such as the ones above, for himself and for clients. The charming painted figurines were first manufactured in the late 1700s in Staffordshire, the center of the English pottery industry. Originally used as economical decoration for the growing middle class, the figures were favors at country fairs around the British Isles. Pastoral scenes depicting life in the countryside with shepherds, hunters, and hunting dogs were popular. Castles, cottages, country churches, and regimental themes were also depicted. Earlier, in the 17th century, the Chinese whetted Western desire for blue-and-white porcelains with export ware for trade with the West. European and British potteries followed suit to fill domestic demand. The two-color palette allows porcelains and pottery of different motifs, such as transfer ware, to be grouped together harmoniously.

COLLECTING staffordshire and blue-and-white

Although tole is the French term for sheet metal, tole lanterns and decorative elements are also associated with English artisans. Tole ware, typically used for lanterns, chandeliers, sconces, bowls, boxes, and cachepots, has been made in Europe and England since the late 18th century. Tole pieces are typically painted black or a rich color such as golden yellow or dark red, then detailed or stenciled with a stylized motif. Tole pieces were particularly popular in the early 19th century—the classically inspired Regency period in England and the Directoire era in France. (Examples here are all 19th-century French.) French urns and bowls tend to have curved shapes and sophisticated motifs. Along with tole, French decorative arts use other matte-finish metals—bronze (such as the lamp base **below**, made from a circa-1860 firedog), iron, and copper. These metals, along with pewter, reflect the burnished surfaces of French interiors.

Living with unpolished, but precious METALS

TWIST
ON
TRADIT

WITH MARY DOUGLAS

The days are gone when a traditional-style interior

meant a prescribed collection of matched furniture

and a formal room arrangement. Today, traditional

ION is as broadly applied as one's personal taste allows.

At the heart of this brand of neotraditionalism is Mary

DRYSDALE

Douglas Drysdale, whose light-filled

rooms reveal both a love of the enduring

Mary Douglas Drysdale

classics and a bent for striking contemporary.

Modernism and neoclassical traditionalism may seem strange aesthetic bedfellows, but to Mary Douglas Drysdale, these diametrically opposed design movements are more closely related than the average mind would suspect. "I happen to find a great similarity between a certain period and type of traditional design and a certain type of modern design," says Drysdale, a designer who lives and works in Washington, D.C., and operates a satellite office in New York.

"Neoclassical design is involved with pure geometry, very straightforward forms, simplicity, and a quiet elegance that is principle driven," she says. "That's also true of much of the best of modern design."

Drysdale, for instance, sees nothing at all unusual in hanging an oil painting by the late archminimalist Donald Judd over a Louis XIV gilt demilune console and then throwing an old American weather vane into the room for good measure. This carefully choreographed crossing of cultural and stylistic lines has the effect of placing the qualities of disparate pieces into greater relief by emphasizing their similarities while appreciating their differences.

"It all works because each piece is all about direct, strong lines, even though they were conceived more than three centuries apart in completely different cultures and under completely different circumstances," says Drysdale, who describes herself as a student of design, learning something new each day. "I tend to focus on the commonality of the elements of the pieces I work with." That is the great lesson of her hallmark synthesis of the best designs of yesteryear with the increasingly streamlined look of today. "Relationships are what allow different pieces of furniture and different art to work together." Elegant and spare "but not pretentious" is how Drysdale describes her rooms, which have a relaxed, put-your-feet-up quality. "I like to give people a sense of the traditional, but updated with a freshness and clarity. For me, tradition is the guide, not the pattern." By which she means that rules, once understood, are meant to be broken—again and again. It's a bit like gardening: Once the formal structure is in place, plants can be added or exchanged without much damage to the overall concept.

"A lot of people say that design isn't rocket science, but they aren't looking at what design encompasses. Every detail, from the fireplace to a stencil on a table to a coatrack, is integral to the design," says the designer, who graduated from two schools known for their rigorous belief in whole-design concepts: the École des

Opposite: In a center hall, a circa-1865 weather vane of a steeplechase horse by Alvin Jewell relaxes the formality of a gold-leaf table and custom neoclassical-style chairs. Architectural shapes meld objects from diverse periods. **Above:** A chair based on the design of English architect Henry Holland is detailed with water gilt.

"I LIKE TO GIVE PEOPLE A SENSE OF TRADITIONAL

BUT UPDATED WITH FRESHNESS AND CLARITY."

In the front sitting area of an elegantly pale double living room, Italian neoclassical gilt chairs with lion's head armrests and paw feet mix with Louis XVI-style gilded bronze and white marble accent tables. A sleek gilt and black lacquered convex mirror hangs above the inlaid marble mantel.

Opposite: Drysdale's architectural sensibilities and refined mix of periods and styles are evident in the beautifully proportioned double living room, visually defined by fluted columns and pilasters. The Corinthian-style capitals and laurel-wreath cornice motif recall the classical roots of modern architecture. The French Régence sconce is gilded bronze. **Above left:** A gilded bull's-eye mirror with ebony trim reflects the serene living room. **Above right:** Art by contemporary painter Donald Judd hangs above a finely detailed, Louis XVI-style demilune. Accent tables are gilded bronze with white marble tops. **Right:** Drysdale chooses every detail and accessory to enrich the planned design. She dresses an antique carved mantel, featuring Greek key inlays, with bronze doré and ebony neoclassical candlesticks from the early 19th century, and a whimsical, modern papier-mâché star.

Beaux-Arts in Paris and the Parsons School of Design in New York. "There is a right solution for the site, a right way to design and build a house and to detail and furnish it. But only after you have the structure and the order, can you take the freedom to break the mold."

Simple and graphic, Drysdale's decors, though far from formulaic, do have certain constant motifs, such as

"PAINTED FURNITURE DOESN'T JUST SIT THERE; IT ENGAGES THE EYE AND BRIGHTENS THE SPACE."

18th-century English, French, and Italian antiques; late-20th-century contemporary art; boldly painted walls; and buoyantly overscaled graphic patterns (checks are a favorite). But there are airy twists that constantly make reference to Drysdale's belief that, no matter how carefully a room is thought out, the end result should look effortless.

Typically, for instance, her curtains are composed of luxurious materials, such as silk or taffeta, but are often left unlined and kept bare of eye-catching passementerie, she

A Swedish pickled gold-leaf chandelier lights the Louis XVI-style parcel gilt mahogany table and Henry Holland-style chairs. Etchings by Claude Lorrain create a subtle backdrop for the 19th-century sphinx and female figure. **Opposite:** The Swedish neoclassical style translates easily into an elegantly simple upholstered bench.

Below: Three prints by Robert Mangold give focus to the living room. Drysdale groups significant art collected by her clients and pairs it with equally bold upholstered pieces. **Left:** A black lacquered metal table anchors the neutral scheme. **Far left:** An architectural fragment repeats the curves of the simple vase and barley twist candlestick.

Above: Neutral walls and upholstery allow art—here a handsomely framed painting by Howard Hodgkin—to be the focal point. Black-and-gold accents, in traditional and contemporary shapes, enrich the scheme. **Right:** Rare weather vanes are a Drysdale signature. **Far right:** An urn in the neoclassical style adds shape and weight to a tabletop.

Subtle gold-leaf stenciling details the cornice in the richly paneled library. Curly maple chairs are based on Swedish neoclassic designs. **Opposite:** An Orientalist oil hangs over the recamier. Orientalist refers to the fanciful paintings of the Near East by 19th-century European artists.

says, "to keep them casual, to keep them simple. It allows one to experience the beauty of the fabric instead of becoming focused on six pompous layers of fringe." And since she opened her office in 1979, one of the designer's signature colors is a cheerful shade of yellow, whose tartness and intensity recall the filling of a lemon meringue pie. Drysdale began using it, she says, "because not a lot of people were using any really strong colors, and I wanted to bring sunlight into a house instead of keeping it at a distance."

Sunlight is one of the designer's primary design tools: the play of light across the carving of a chair leg, the sparkle of the brass edge of a dining table, and especially how light works its magic when paired with painted furniture. "I have a cultural love affair with painted furniture: French, Italian, Scandinavian, Russian," says the designer, whose own home in Washington, D.C., is a casually elegant showcase of neoclassical furnishings set against eye-popping color. "The forms of 18th-century furniture are formal, but when the forms are painted, they take on a curious dual quality: crisp but humble, and

Drysdale pairs contemporary art, such as this print by Richard Diebenkorn, with comfortable family furnishings and folk art. **Opposite:** In a formal setting, she's adept at finding unifying elements between a Donald Judd painting, a Louis XVI-style demilune, and a classically inspired urn.

"NEOCLASSICAL IS INVOLVED WITH GEOMETRY;
THAT'S ALSO TRUE OF THE BEST OF MODERN."

ANNIE LEIBOVITZ

CEZANNE   JOHN REWALD   ABRAMS

sculptural. There's a tension there that appeals to me. Painted furniture doesn't just sit there, doing nothing. It engages the eye and brightens the space."

For similar reasons, she has a proclivity for utilizing stencils instead of wallpaper in her interiors. The edge of a

"THE TOUCH OF THE HAND IS IMPORTANT TO ME; YOU ARE BUYING A

pickled parquet floor might be ringed with golden, stylized acanthus leaves and tendrils, for instance, or the drawer pull of a small white side table flanked with a pair of honeybees in full flight. Handmade quilts are another important element in her work. Either antique or designed by her own office, they are tossed insouciantly across the end of a comfortable upholstered chaise longue or drip off an antique daybed to create a river of color. "The touch of the hand is important in my work," Drysdale says, "because you are buying a piece of someone else's mind and creativity. You get order and spontaneity in one simple gesture."

For the classically trained Drysdale, a house is a living entity, not just a series of discrete spaces. "I like to deal with a house as a whole, as a spirit, rather than as a series of individual rooms," the designer says. Though an unrepentant neoclassicist at heart, she has been greatly influenced by the work of Frank Lloyd Wright and the Scottish architect Charles Rennie Mackintosh, primarily by their belief that architecture and design must work together to

Right: Skirted slipcovers and Drysdale's signature bolster-style pillows relax neoclassical chairs in a breakfast room. **Opposite top:** George III-style chairs add elegant seating to the kitchen's banquette and stenciled pedestal table. **Opposite bottom:** The designer warms casual settings with folk art. American weather vanes, such as this gilded piece, are favorites.

PIECE OF SOMEONE'S MIND."

Drysdale designed this bedroom with a mix of European-inspired styles based on the sleek lines and curves of the neoclassical period. The Empire-style settee works with a stenciled armoire in the style of Swedish furniture. **Opposite:** An American folk art quilt contributes its own graphic punch.

achieve a comfortable totality. "A house has a character that wants to be expressed and should have a vocabulary that should be evident," she adds. "Rooms don't exist in a vacuum. You have to be aware of adjacent rooms and how they relate. The transitions between the rooms should be seamless, the way a great ballet is. One moves from one movement to the next without a jarring feeling but instead a feeling of logic, comfort, and clarity of direction."

Mad-mix decoration can be comfortable, she says, but only to a limited degree. "As a decorating style, eclecticism has been popular for the last 10 years, but when it is done only for the sake of mixing, I find it wildly disorienting." So it comes as no surprise that the exuberant interiors of the mid- and late-19th century leave Drysdale cold. "I'm not a great fan of anything Victorian. Most of the time, it's just overwhelmingly busy. It is not a period of design with which I feel a great deal of comfort. But I would be happy to do it for a client—if I could make it relevant for today."

Opposite: Silk taffeta draperies, elegantly simple in design and exquisite in execution, soften the views. The custom desk is in the Louis XVI style, a natural transition to the architectural furniture of the neoclassic period. **Left:** Drysdale creates comfort and ease by relaxing austere pieces, such as this gilded side chair, with a flirty skirt and bolster-style pillow. **Above left:** Framed pages from Henri Matisse's *Poems Charles d' Orleans* create a beautifully subtle focal point for the light-filled master suite. The accent table, with cabriole legs, is a Drysdale-designed piece, delicately stenciled with lighthearted honeybees. The mix of the simple and the grand infuses her projects with a relaxed liveliness. **Above:** A sunburst mirror works as art in this serene master bath. Marble tiles and gold-plated fixtures contribute to the opulent ambience, while a skylight adds cheerful natural light.

Mary Douglas Drysdale is a lifelong student of design. With her background in architecture, art history, and product design, she gravitates to the strong geometric forms that unite interiors and furnishings across time and cultures. Of particular note in her work is the pairing of the neoclassical period in architecture and decorative arts, sparked by the discoveries of the Roman cities of Pompeii and Herculeum in the mid-18th century, with the pared-down strength of 20th-century design and art. Stars, **above left,** are recurring motifs, as are the circles and squares of a mosaic, **above center,** that recall its classical origins. The designer, who is well versed in the history of design, chose the familiarity of the timeless Greek key pattern, **below left,** for a room that unites the ancient, the neoclassic, and the contemporary. She is equally adept at incorporating swags and fleur-de-lis motifs, **above right** and **below center** and **right,** associated with more ornate eras.

DETAILS applied to architectural elements

As she refines interiors to settings of spare elegance, Drysdale raises traditional stenciling to a beautifully wrought art form. She works with artists to design and execute the motifs that reflect the waves of classical revival in the decorative arts. Stenciled details illustrate her interest in European design. The chest, **above center,** in warm yellow and white recalls subtle Scandinavian influences seen in the designer's work. The classical and neoclassical converge in patterns such as the stylized leaves on a black table, **above left,** and the delicate border of the bound sisal rug, **above right.** The geometry of the circles and straight lines in both pieces is a recurring theme in Drysdale's work. Also recurring is her well-known playful signature of a stylized honeybee, **below right**, which alludes to her passion for fine American folk art as well as Scandinavian design. Always discreet, she relaxes her subtle motifs, **below left** and **below center,** for more painterly detailing.

Aging furnishings with painted-on STENCILS

UPDATING
AMERIC
CLASSICS

WITH GARY

Classic furniture and decorative arts that reflect

a love of heritage and a respect for fine

Gary McBournie

craftsmanship are great starting points for

long-lasting rooms. Gary McBournie adds to this mix

an array of spry color schemes, playful patterns,

AN

and contemporary art as he creates relaxed

interiors with undeniable all-American appeal. His

rooms combine a love of home with lively style.

M C B O U R N I E

Classic American furniture and decorative arts are the starting points for the lively, youthful interiors of Boston interior designer Gary McBournie. With his sure touch for appealing color and fresh fabrics, classic 19th-century furniture and art are wonderfully incorporated into homes for family living. The love of American history and culture is natural for McBournie, who grew up and studied art and design in

"I ADD COLOR AND PRINTED FABRICS THAT WOULDN'T HAVE BEEN USED IN THE 19TH CENTURY."

New England. "I've always been drawn to patina for furniture, objects, my everyday surroundings," says McBournie. "I can't imagine living with everything new."

As a young designer, McBournie worked with a prestigious Boston firm, R. FitzGerald and Company, known for fine traditional work and discerning clients. "I started with clients who had their own family pieces and, many times, their own art and collections," he says. "I found I enjoyed reusing clients' own possessions. For me, the best client is one who comes with a sense of personal style, some kind of good collection, and maybe some wonderful family pieces or paintings. That all breathes life into a home."

Breathing life is what McBournie loves and does best. Despite his eye for antiques, paintings, and decorative arts, his approach is personal, not antiquarian. He incorporates

Classic New England motifs, such as the Windsor chairs and bench, and a rag rug, are updated with pale walls and fishermen's net fabric on black iron drapery rods. Boxed, piped seat cushions are made from old quilt squares and vintage fabrics.

Opposite: In a dining room with ever-changing coastal views, an electrified lantern, converted from a 19th-century bell jar (or cloche) originally designed to protect plants, hangs above the pine farm table. Spatterware plates detail the wall. **Left:** Above the sideboard, a hanging French plate rack organizes stick-cut and spongeware from Wales and Scotland. **Above left:** Neutral surfaces and upholstery provide a sophisticated, updated backdrop for fine European and Oriental antiques. Off-white cotton canvas refreshes a classic wing chair and pleated drapery treatment. The chinoiserie table is more practical with a glass top. **Above right:** The French barrel chair, slipcovered in canvas and detailed with clever buttoned tabs, blends with the stone shade of strié wallpaper. Below the ornate painted and gilded Italian mirror, a carved Italian chest displays crystal candle lamps and a lacquered Japanese box.

"I PARTICULARLY LIKE TO

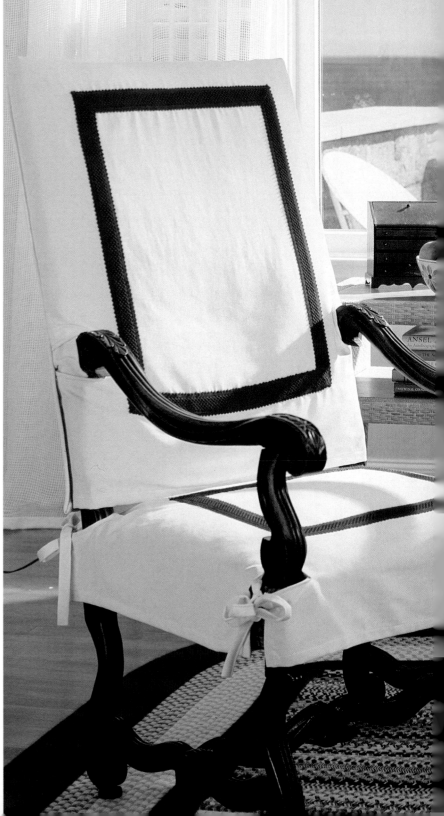

the furnishings of the past, particularly fine 19th-century American antiques, into rooms designed for the present.

In some settings, McBournie chooses intense color for walls; in others, where decorative arts and furniture are paramount, he works with an updated neutral palette. In

INTERJECT RED AND YELLOW INTO TRADITIONAL INTERIORS."

every case, creating personal, inviting spaces with fabrics, art, and family treasures is a signature of his inviting style.

"The museum reproductions of supposedly 18th- or 19th-century rooms isn't what I do," McBournie says. "They don't allow you to live in them. We don't live in 1800, and we don't need to pretend we do." Rather, his approach is to give a hint of a familiar period feel without being locked into a strict re-creation. "I add color and printed cotton fabrics that wouldn't have been used in the 19th century. I like them because they warm and relax rooms. Traditional design doesn't need to mean a lot of boring brown furniture. It's far more interesting to take things from the past that have meaning to you and add some paint and fresh color." The classic appeal is timeless.

As a collector and lover of tradition, McBournie prizes things from the past, particularly early-19th-century American furniture and decorative arts, arranged with English and French pieces. "I like furniture made in New

Left: The daybed's checkerboard fabric pairs with the contemporary woven rattan table and turn-of-the-century armchair. **Opposite top:** The antique quilt has the graphic impact of contemporary art. A sea captain's camphor-wood trunk serves as the coffee table. **Opposite bottom:** Framed regimental needlepoint, known as "woolies," hang above an open-twist table.

An off-white duck-covered sofa gives seating without dominating the scheme in this seaside entry hall. The model boat relaxes the mood; a seagrass rug, cut-down pine farm table, and mirror enhance the airy feel. The country French fruitwood chest and side table warm with mellow tones.

England and along the East Coast south to Baltimore from around 1820 to 1840, the American response in the Federal period to the Regency style in England," he says. "The furniture made then in the United States was beautifully crafted but a little heavier and more robust than the English pieces. There's a life and character to it that appeals to me. Pieces, such as small sideboards and highboys, are wonderful in their workmanship and difficult to find." The dark woods, often mahogany, give pieces of the period the patina associated with classic traditional design.

Painted 19th-century furniture contributes, too, to the warm mix and charm of traditional interiors. "I enjoy using American wedding furniture pieces, which are usually white with gilding," adds McBournie. "They're as fun to use as they are light, lively pieces. And I'm also drawn to pieces with the rustic, worn finishes of old paints, in reds, greens, and mustard shades."

In his own relaxed fashion, the designer often mixes painted and dark woods or even light pine in casual rooms. In formal settings, black lacquered accent chairs and gilded mirrors enhance the sophisticated schemes.

American and English chairs of the early 19th century are used as accent pieces. For his own lively take on traditional design, McBournie re-covers or slipcovers these classic styles in bright, casual fabrics or mixes plaids, prints, and solids for design interest. As a designer for family living, he isn't averse to incorporating well-designed and crafted reproductions into his projects. The key, he adds, is to find reproduction dining or accent chairs in the styles and finishes appropriate to the rooms he designs.

McBournie also carefully selects both antique and reproduction upholstered sofas and chairs. A master of working with comfortable pieces, he's known for his signature dressmaker details. He adds an array of passementerie, fabric trims, covered buttons, and pleats to solids and prints.

Serious antiques, including late-19th-century Scottish great-hall chairs, relax with updated slipcovers detailed with tailored decorative tapes and trims. Depending on the project, McBournie may opt for a fine English-made printed fabric or for a sturdy, natural cotton canvas for upholstery and slipcovers.

This creative mix of fabrics and styles seems contemporary. But in reality, New England rooms of the early 19th century would likely have contained imported English and French fabrics, decorative arts, and furniture as well as American furnishings. "I add English and French furniture and sometimes Italian because I enjoy them," the designer explains. "But that was a common thing to do in the 19th

Opposite: Slipcovers simplify turn-of-the-century great-hall chairs, thought to be Scottish. The wall-hung English Act of Parliament clock contrasts with the Dutch-Baroque-inspired table. **Above:** Delicate antique delft graces the pristine mantel.

"TAKE THINGS FROM THE PAST THAT HAVE
MEANING AND ADD SOME COLOR AND PAINT."

In the kitchen and adjoining breakfast room, painted and stained diamond-patterned floors recall old New England houses. The trompe l'oeil cabinet doors translate a French decorative painting technique into lighthearted American style. **Right:** An iron chandelier illuminates the reproduction pedestal table and ladder-back chairs.

century, too. Many pieces were imported, a lot of English and more French, even in New England, than many people think. It's important to keep in mind when you work with traditional styles that houses were never done completely in fine

"I ADD ENGLISH AND FRENCH FURNITURE AND SOMETIMES ITALIAN BECAUSE I ENJOY USING THEM."

American furniture and decorative arts." Especially along the Atlantic coast, merchants and professional families traveled to Europe and had business and family connections abroad. At the same time, the lively export trade up and down the eastern seaboard exchanged raw American whaling, timber, and agricultural products for finished British and European fabrics, clothing, furniture, pottery, porcelains, and china. Trade with the Far East introduced export ware.

For example, McBournie says, compared to the British Isles, Europe, and the Far East, little porcelain and pottery were made in the United States in the early 19th century, but much was imported. "The porcelains in a New England home,

Pale walls highlight English chinoiserie furniture and lacquered accessories. Simply framed for impact, German botanical prints are by Basil Besler, who worked in the late 16th and early 17th centuries. **Opposite:** A mirror updates the 19th-century shell-art picture frame; a French bench is circa 1900.

In this master bedroom nook, a chaise longue and French armchair share the American Empire drop-leaf reading table. A Dutchess of Windsor-style pleated shade dresses up a glass table lamp.

Above: In a bedroom designed around Oriental fans, an upholstered headboard converts two Italian twin beds on hoofed feet into one king-size bed. Stripes in three widths reinforce the palette. **Right:** Topiary wallpaper and a detailed sink dress a powder room. **Far right:** Bristol glass bottles and a terry-cloth-slipcovered chair enliven a master bath.

for example, would have been blue and white from the Far East, beautifully painted pieces from France, or spatterware from Wales, England, or Scotland."

Spatterware, which features simple, colorful designs, illustrates how well 19th-century pottery and accessories fit with current decorating. McBournie's work recalls the pottery's graphic, vibrant motifs by pairing bright wall colors with simplified shapes and forms. "I like white woodwork and trim throughout a house, set off by contrasting walls, not just a bland palette," he notes. "And I'm comfortable with blocks of intense color on walls, which give a strong quality to design. I particularly like to interject red and yellow, when it works, into traditional interiors. Intense color gives traditional furniture, which tends to be dark, a more spirited attitude."

Working in vibrant palettes with walls—sometimes painted, sometimes papered—as colorful backdrops, McBournie enjoys introducing painted floors in bold checkerboard patterns. And he incorporates another classic of American style, braided rugs, into contemporary interpretations. "I design braided rugs in bright colors and stripes, rather than necessarily using old rugs," the designer says. "That gives clearer colors than you would find in a rug that has faded over time, and braided rugs are more

relaxed than Orientals." Although he does use fine Oriental rugs when they add color and texture to settings, the designer also likes the more pared-down feel of sisal or even bare wood floors in more formal rooms.

Quilts, too, bridge the traditional and contemporary in McBournie's work. "I consider quilts as art with graphic, colorful qualities," the designer says. "I like to hang quilts as major pieces, just as you would colorful contemporary paintings," he explains. Quilts work in rooms with high ceilings, where groupings of paintings would be busy or large, traditional paintings difficult to find.

In keeping with his love for vintage pieces, McBournie says he prefers the detailing and history of antique quilts to new ones. "The really good old ones have enough bold pattern and color that they look contemporary, yet they still are fine, collectible antiques," he says. "That's why I like to use them." He also enjoys the freedom of introducing contemporary abstract art into traditional settings. "Contemporary art works beautifully with 18th- and 19th-century furniture, as they respond to one another in their simplicity. I've found abstract paintings with bold colors work the best. The pairing brings new life in an unconventional way to antiques, and it gives contemporary art a little more warmth."

Above: Rare Redouté botanical prints hang in stair-step fashion over the decoupaged sideboard. Delft plates visually bridge the elements. **Opposite:** Pale, subtle backdrops give a fresh approach to antiques. The Regency mirror reflects the Venetian chandelier above the 18th-century American Chippendale chairs and Empire dining table.

Antique quilts, collected by the owners, set the cheerful peachy pink-and-white color scheme for a guest bedroom that pairs candy stripes and a sprigged floral wallpaper. Duvets feature covered, contrasting buttons. **Opposite:** Weathered by age and seasons, an antique iron garden urn on an entry-hall table spills over with a collection of delicate shells.

"I'VE ALWAYS BEEN DRAWN TO PATINA FOR FURNITURE, OBJECTS, EVEN MY SURROUNDINGS."

Opposite: Emphasizing the setting and an American oil painting, a playful novelty print becomes the armchair's summer slipcover. Majolica pitchers are grouped for maximum impact. **Left:** McBournie begins his color palette with blocks of color in solids, or as illustrated by the piped yellow sofa, in subtle stripes. He repeats the colors with a play of carefully chosen prints, such as the nautical motif, and with stripes, checks, and florals. **Above left:** Barley-twist chairs, renewed with whitewash and two upholstery fabrics, pair with a crackle-finish pedestal breakfast table, lit by a twig-motif chandelier. With the painted, diamond-patterned floor beneath, the update lightens traditional pieces. **Above right:** A collection of majolica plates hung around the mirror inspired the fresh, clear colors for this much-used family room. A matching pair of sofas maximizes seating in a living area.

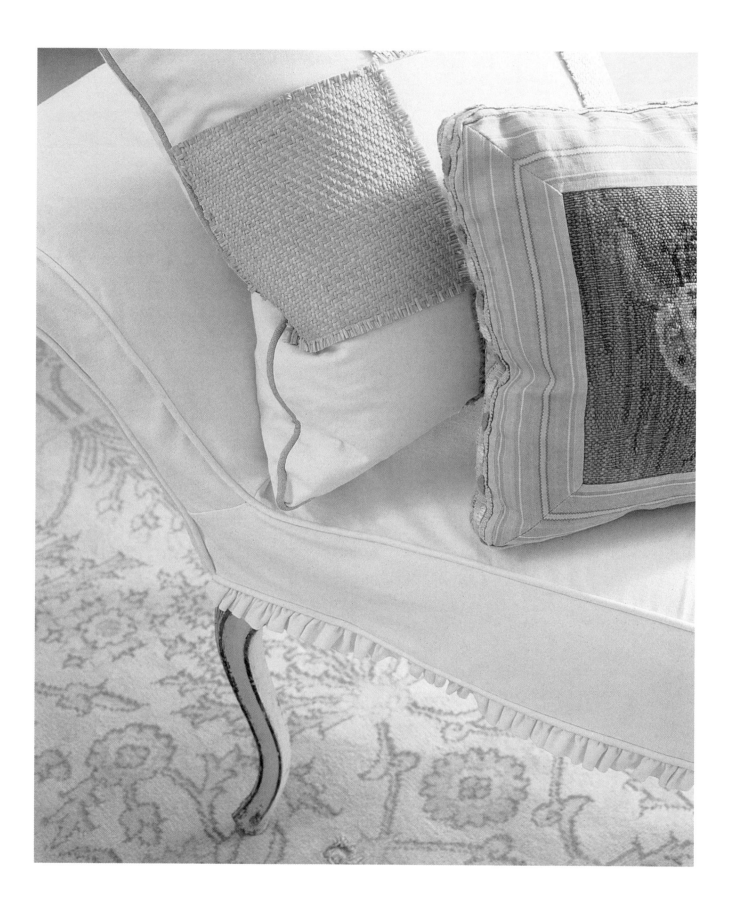

The magic of traditional interior design is in the minutest, most exacting details for Gary McBournie. The designer begins with handsome, often English, fabrics, then adds his own exquisite dressmaker touches. In the sophisticated living room, **opposite,** pillows made from squares of raffia and antique fabrics add interest and comfort to a turn-of-the-century slipcovered bench detailed with ruched trim. A collector of antique American quilts, McBournie often plans room schemes around the treasured textiles, **below left** and **right.** This love of fine textiles and fabrication carries over to the slipcovers he designs to dress traditional chairs in light summer fabrics, **below center.** Casual, tie-on slipcovers, tucked and pleated to fit, illustrate the designer's standards. **Above,** attention to detail extends to a mix of fabrics on chairs, to tabs and buttons that secure slipcovers smoothly in place, and to piped, tie-on boxed chair cushions that update Windsor-style chairs.

Tailoring furnishings with dressmaker DETAILS

INDULGENT
COMFO

WITH THOMAS

Many rooms are comfortable, but those that are

luxuriously comfortable indulge their occupants with

R**T** elements that speak to all of the senses. Fabrics that

combine pretty colors and touchable textures; fine

BARTLETT

furniture, beautiful in form and finish, that coddles

the human form; and art and antiques that

evoke emotions and perhaps memories. These are

Thomas Bartlett

the kinds of rooms that Thomas Bartlett designs.

Before the first color or fabric swatch is chosen for a client's home, Napa Valley designer Thomas Bartlett has worked with the architect, contractor, landscape architect, lighting designer, and fine artisans on every facet, large and small, of the plan. Many conversations and hours later, the result will be an exquisitely finished, refined home that reflects the interests and passions of the owners, but *not*, the designer emphasizes, easily identifiable trademarks of his design.

"I've learned over the years not to rubber-stamp myself on clients," explains Bartlett, who established his own firm

"IT WORKED PARTICULARLY WELL TO USE ONLY ANTIQUE CHINESE RUGS."

in 1968. "As my first jobs were in what was then a small community, I wanted to be creative for the clients and give each one something unique and different. Later, when I started working on jobs around the country, I still saw my role as taking clients where they wanted to go, rather than imposing my personal taste and interests on them." Unlike some designers who are known for a look or trademark palette, Bartlett works with what he calls preferences for styles, finishing materials, furnishings, and art. The results are inviting, always-sophisticated homes, but never easily identifiable palettes or decorative arts.

His own life experiences have helped him to be comfortable with multiple styles. "I grew up on a Napa cattle ranch and raised pedigreed swine," he says. Balancing this pas-

Bartlett designed the pediment-topped, mahogany armoire with gilded pilasters to conceal the family room's television and stereo. A classic, symmetrical arrangement of matching sofas with an ottoman maximizes seating. The rug is antique Chinese.

91

The palette of blue and yellow enlivens the living room's formal furnishings and trimmed silk and damask fabrics. A hand-painted cornice crowns the yellow walls, which have a strié finish. **Opposite:** A collection of sterling vases and trophy cups illustrates the impact of family collections.

THE ENGLISH PARK SUSAN LASDUN

"FOR THIS HOME, I INTRODUCED WARM YELLOWS INTO THE BLUE-AND-WHITE PALETTE."

toral existence was a deep passion for painting. After Bartlett attended the California College of Arts and Crafts, he worked at the Hearst Castle in San Simeon. But it wasn't until a fellow Californian, interior designer Elizabeth Carter Green, lured Bartlett back to Napa Valley that he found himself in the world of interior design. Through his collaboration with Green and later on his own, Bartlett was exposed to an array of fine antiques, art, architecture, and varied decorative arts.

Seemingly disparate influences attract Bartlett and inspire his work. "I've spent a great deal of time in Italy, and I love 18th- and 19th-century Italian furniture," says the designer. In the same breath, he also comments, "that is just one facet of my work, however." The art climate of the mid-century imparted a modernist direction to his work, albeit subtly. "I was interested in what was cutting-edge design (in the 1960s)," he says. "The San Francisco area attracted contemporary artists, and over the years, I had clients with major contemporary collections."

By the time he expanded his design business to a retail shop and studio in downtown Napa in 1984, his showroom included European antique furniture and decorative arts and investment-quality contemporary art. The mix is symbolic of Bartlett's interests and design strengths—and

the sophistication of his well-traveled clients.

As examples of how he works, he points to two extensive projects that reflect the interests of their owners. "One started when the owner purchased an 18th-century French paneled room," he says. "Their house was an unremarkable shed-roof contemporary. There was nothing French about it." But six years and much remodeling and redecorating later, the house is decidedly Continental, with French doors to the gardens, elegant window treatments, and fine antique furniture and art. The lengthy project is indicative of how Bartlett guides a project from start to finish, working with the appropriate professionals and fine craftspeople.

For another traditional project, Bartlett started with two givens—the client's collection of American and English antiques and the owner's love of blue-and-white. "She had seen a house I did years ago in a blue-and-white scheme and remembered it," the designer says. "But the public rooms needed to be warmer, so for this home, I introduced warm yellows into the blue-and-white palette. We decorated the bedrooms in blues, ivories, and off-whites. We have two related, but distinctive palettes for the house, which works very well for the family."

In keeping with this home's antiques and picturesque

Opposite: Antique Italian dining chairs pair with a turned-leg table in a cozy dining room. The antique English flip-top game table fits into the tight corner and works as an extra server. **Above:** In a symmetrical arrangement of pairs, framed Chinese fabric squares flank an antique mirror. Urns and jars are arranged on the Sheraton sideboard.

European country-house-style architecture. Bartlett planned paint finishes that quickly aged the major remodeling. "I enjoy working with artists on decorative finishes." he says. "We used hand-distressed and hand-glazed finishes to give the walls the appearance of 150 years of loving care and wear." The motifs were influenced by 18th-century painting and stenciling. but everything is originally designed. rather than being copies. In a similar approach. the borders are hand-drawn and painterly. rather than being tightly rendered. "I like painted details to bear the mark of the artist's hand." Bartlett says.

The blue-dominated scheme for the paint detailing pointed to the use of antique Chinese rugs. Unlike

"WE LOOK FOR FABRICS TO GIVE A FRESH APPEARANCE TO

the reds of patterned Oriental rugs or the pale tones of Aubussons. the vivid blues of Chinese rugs fit with the blue-and-white palette. "Selecting rugs for an entire house like this takes time." Bartlett says. "We spent four months and worked with various dealers to find just the right 13 rugs we needed. I find it effective to limit the styles of rug in a home. It worked well. with the two palettes and antiques. to use only antique Chinese." The choice and careful selection of rugs exemplifies Bartlett's patience in taking the time needed to help clients

Right: Fresh paint and striped fabric update Victorian chairs on this sun-dappled loggia. The Oriental garden seat alludes to the terrace outside. **Opposite top:** Woven contemporary seating mixes with bamboo tables for a convivial grouping. **Opposite bottom:** Artfully aged walls create the backdrop for an English walnut bureau, circa 1730, and a Regency-period Sheraton chair.

THE ANTIQUES WE ARE USING."

A lively floral sets the scheme for the master bedroom. Shades of blue blend from light to deeper tints from the carpet to the striped walls. To avoid overmatching, a skirted table pairs with an English chest and collected export-ware urns are lamp bases.

Above: Hand-painted motifs, including the costumed monkey, and delicately scaled antiques set a youthful mood in a bedroom for young sisters. Beds are freshened with an antique pine-and-gold finish. **Right:** A mix of pillows in three sizes invites reading and relaxing. **Far right:** A lively plaid and lighthearted novelty print energize family antiques.

make the best decorating choices and the wisest, long-term design decisions.

From the rugs, Bartlett built the fabric scheme with florals, stripes, and solids in an array of cottons, linens, and silks. "We look to the fabrics to give a fresh appearance to the upholstery and antiques we are using," he notes. "This client has beautiful, classic dark wood pieces, and the fabrics give them a new life." In addition to the 18th- and early-19th-century pieces, Bartlett also relaxed Victorian chairs, now used for loggia dining, with a lively stripe. Lush in their colorations, fabrics are also generously applied. Dressmaker details and trims finish window treatments, table skirts, and pillows. Bedrooms feature over-scaled hangings, luxurious in design and yardage. Beautiful, opulent window treatments and skirted vanities also contribute to the sense of ease and retreat both for the master suite and for guest bedrooms.

Regardless of the client or the environment, Bartlett has preferences for the surfacing materials he employs. "When I use carpet, I like flat, tight loop, as it's serviceable, and area rugs can be layered over it. I like to use the same color when carpeting is in more than one room. And when I'm doing a job where wood flooring is involved, if it's appropriate, I like No. 2 grade walnut. I bleach it to a lighter color, then have it sealed and waxed for a weathered appearance."

In a dining room with a view, subtly striped damask wallpaper adds pattern and color, while windows are uncovered. To heighten the French feel, an 18th-century crystal-and-gilt frame chandelier lights a carved provincial walnut table. **Opposite:** A mix of pillows invites guests to gather on the banquette.

Opposite: Delicate French chairs, here a pair of fauteuil armchairs and a comfortable bergère with ottoman, add comfortable seating without overpowering a private sitting area. The chandelier is rock crystal and silvered iron. Above: A hand-sewn window treatment, made from silk squares, calms the mood in a master suite. The late-18th-century Venetian hanging corner cupboard is one of a pair. Above right: Striped wallpaper provides the tailored backdrop for a poufed window treatment and a feminine, skirted custom vanity in this boudoir-style bedroom. The daybed, three-legged table, and Louis XVI-style dressing stool are French. The candlestick lamp and crystal accessories enhance the delicate look. Right: In an opulent master bath retreat of marble tile and curved cabinetry, the mirrored chandelier diffuses light. A chinoiserie frame highlights antique glass.

When stone is an option, he specifies a pale fossil stone from Germany, which is installed sealed, not polished. Whatever the flooring, he prefers to keep materials to no more than two different surfaces to avoid distractions.

From overall design to the smallest detail, Bartlett's preference is for the long-term, not the trendy or quickly

"I SPENT A GREAT DEAL OF TIME IN ITALY; I LOVE 18TH-AND 19TH-CENTURY ITALIAN FURNITURE."

dated. "I don't work in a certain period, although I love to work with furniture from the 18th century and art from the 20th. I've worked on houses decorated in the 1920s and 1930s that were intact with wonderful bones. My job wasn't to redesign, but to refresh. I came back and based new things on very fine foundations. When you have timeless design, you can do that. That's the kind of design and the kind of homes I hope I do."

In a living room of grand proportions, a painted Chinese planter visually separates two seating groupings. Two pairs of Italian armchairs, with the original painted finishes, provide versatile seating. Chinese garden seats in the Famille Rose pattern accent as decorative tables. **Opposite:** A boar's-hide ottoman serves as the coffee table.

Thomas Bartlett approaches interiors from the sensibilities of both a well-traveled artist and an art historian. Under his scrutiny, hand-painted finishes transcend wall decoration to become highly decorative art. The subtle, shadowed effect of rusticated stone, **opposite**, recalling trompe l'oeil, alludes to the classic villas of the designer's beloved Italy, as well as wine-country architecture. Strié and glazing techniques give new walls the well-worn patina of age, **above right** and **below right**. Painterly scrollwork with intricate shadowing adds the allusion of depth to cornice friezes, **above left** and **below center**. The stylized motifs of the Orient that have inspired European styles for centuries are seen in Bartlett's designs, too, as the detailed bracket, **above center**, illustrates. And the romance of pastoral landscapes, appropriate to the valley he calls home, translates into the fanciful scenes of exotic animals and well-dressed monkeys he commissions for cabinet doors, **below left**.

Adding interest with painted FINISHES

PRETTY AND POLISH

WITH PAULA

The phrase "pretty as a picture" never loses its

relevancy when it comes to creating

appealing, successful interiors. With a trained

Paula Perlini

artist's eye toward balancing furniture selection

and arrangement with her natural flair for

color and finishing touches, Paula Perlini designs

ED

warm, family-friendly rooms that literally

sit up and pose gracefully for the camera.

PERLINI

As all students and lovers of interior design know, there is no better way to train your eye to distinguish between brava and beauty than seeing both firsthand. New York interior designer Paula Perlini, who spent her student years in Italy and Switzerland, is an excellent case in point. "The great museums and architectural wonders of Rome were my classroom," she says of her education in sculpture and art history at the Accademia di Belle Arti in Rome.

But as all students and lovers of interior design also know, applying an understanding of good design to a room takes another set of skills, one that comes with practice and patience. Returning home from Rome to Cincinnati, Perlini worked for an established interior designer and then formed her own decorating firm. Ultimately, fate would call her to New York. The renowned interior designer Mark Hampton offered her a job at his Manhattan firm, and Perlini eagerly accepted.

"I had always wanted to work with Mark," notes Perlini, and under Hampton's guidance, she polished her skills. "Mark was a fabulous teacher because he knew so much about the history of furniture and the various periods of decoration and architecture. He had a photographic memory and could recall exactly how a room he'd seen ten years ago looked and was furnished. He also was masterful at furniture arrangement."

During her tenure at Hampton's firm, Perlini worked on the decoration of Blair House, one of four historic landmark buildings in Washington, D.C., that serves as the Presidential guest house for visiting heads of state. After nearly a decade with Hampton, Perlini formed her own Manhattan-based design business. She quickly became known for her easy way with classic furniture forms, gracious room arrangements, and masterful detailing.

Perlini's rooms always revolve around a well-thought-out furniture plan for collecting and arranging. Many of her clients have collections, art, or family pieces to use as the starting point for design projects. For others, she oversees the thoughtful melding of furnishings and decorative arts from different styles and periods. The layering through the years reflects how families have traditionally furnished and decorated their homes.

Because her projects are geared to how families live and enjoy their homes, Perlini pays particular attention to choosing comfortable furnishings. "I put a lot of furniture in a room, so it has to be well placed," she says. Seating areas are always proportional to a room, but in larger spaces Perlini often clusters two to three groupings for

Opposite: A velvet love seat adds extra seating in a dining room with an English pedestal table and Queen Anne-style chairs. The antique French lantern illuminates the richly detailed Oriental rug, Italian mirror, Imari plates and charger, and export porcelains. **Above:** Stacked boxes create visual interest under an antique English Chippendale tea table.

A mahogany English sofa table, with a cast-ball-footed peg tankard, finds contemporary use as a console table—and as an extra table for an apartment without a formal dining room. An antique English cellarette wine holder serves as the coffee table and balances the ornate Italian gilt mirror.

easy, convivial conversation areas. Traffic patterns are implied by the arrangements, rather than firmly delineated. And extra chairs and ottomans are included to accommodate good-size gatherings for family and social occasions.

"I assume everyone is going to be in a room at the same time—the adults, the kids, friends," Perlini says. Thus she uses a range of upholstered shapes to provide comfort for various tastes. "For people who want back support and don't want to struggle out of a deep sofa, I like to include a high-back chair in a living room," she says. "I also love to add slipper chairs because they are small and versatile—you can move them around a room when there are groups of people." Comfortable upholstered furniture isn't limited to the living room. "I also like to put upholstery in dining rooms and bedrooms, so there is always a comfortable place to sit." Examples include decorative antique settees for formal dining rooms, and curvy recamiers or chaise longues for master bedrooms.

Variety and symmetry may seem to be design opposites, but Perlini uses both to her advantage. "I like a variety of furniture shapes and forms, with some pieces bigger, others smaller—some low, some high," she notes. For example, the designer often places a high piece, such as a tea table, in front of one sofa and a low table, such as a lac-

quered Oriental piece, in front of another. But within this mix, she also imposes a subtle, well-ordered balance with symmetrical pairs. "I like pairs, but I do them so that the room does not look matchy-matchy," Perlini explains. "I might have two pairs of open armchairs opposite each other in a room to create a balanced layout. But to keep the scheme from looking dull, I use two different pairs. The pairs of chairs will be compatible shapes and proportions, but not identical. On a similar note, I try to use two sofas in a living room—but they will not necessarily be mirror images of each other—to give the look and feel I want."

In a Perlini-designed room, quality upholstered pieces, whether antique or reproduction, are essential. "I encourage my clients to buy good custom upholstery because they'll have it for a lifetime," she says. "They can always re-cover it or slipcover it and shift it around to other rooms, and the piece will last for decades. There are some classic upholstered shapes that I like to use. One is the Bridgewater chair, which is a deep-seated club chair. Another is a sofa with a high, rolled arm and back that are the same height all the way around." When she finds them, Perlini adds antique upholstered pieces, such as an Edwardian club chair or a Victorian slipper chair. And she scours shops for

Opposite: Antiques work hard in city apartments. In a mahogany-paneled library sitting room, the writing table and Chippendale armchair contribute to the visual openness.
Above: The Regency drop-leaf table opens up to serve six when the library is the dining room. Upholstered side chairs work well when used for dining or for reading.

117

comfortable antique chairs or chaises to copy in updated fabrics and decorative trims, tapes, or braids.

Perlini believes such finishing touches for draperies, as well as upholstery, can make or break a room. "With curtains and upholstery, simplicity is key when it comes to the details," she says. "Too many details can make a room look amateurish—like a design-school project." And regardless of how well a finishing touch is designed, its execution is essential to its effect. "Excellent craftsmanship is part of the success of a well-designed room," Perlini insists. She stresses the need to use the best workrooms and fabricators, even when the application seems simple, to get the pleasing classic touches she demands for her design jobs.

Perlini's advice on color is as precise as her feelings about furnishings. "I encourage my clients to use color," the designer says. "Color enhances our environments. Color makes collections and art stand out. Put a gold frame on a colored wall or a black frame with a white mat against a colored wall, and they really pop. I love red, and I love to use red or reddish tones in dining rooms, libraries, even bedrooms. Red makes a room warm and inviting."

Other favorites include dark, rich hues such as bottle green and deep eggplant. Such strong colors also trigger the addition of white to a room's color scheme: "I always use white woodwork because it makes the core color stand out even more," she notes.

While blue is evident in some of Perlini's inviting rooms.

Right: Painted sisal in the style of Sultanbad carpet relaxes chic French-style chairs. **Opposite top:** A marble-top, mahogany American Empire dresser offers substantial style and bedroom storage. A Victorian-era wicker chair and recamier add interest. **Opposite bottom:** Upholstered pieces pair with antique tables. The Chinese export star-motif porcelain keeps the look light.

Below: Apricot glazed walls warm a living room enriched with pale upholstery and collected 20th-century art. Left: A rare oyster-wood veneered William and Mary chest-on-stand, from the 18th century, displays blue-and-white export ware. Far left: Hand-painted striped walls update the mix of English and Irish antiques, including the English hall chair.

Above: A damask slipcover and oversize cut-velvet checkerboard pillows introduce casual elegance into an art collector's living room. Dutch old masters, in gilt and old wood frames, hang above. Right: A bright floral wallpaper relaxes the master bedroom. Far right: A handsomely framed old-master drawing, on a stand, gives a different perspective.

it usually plays second or third fiddle to other colors. "Blue can be very cold unless you put a lot of white with it," says the designer. She gives a recent client's residence on Martha's Vineyard as an example for choosing colors other than this perennial summer-home favorite.

The homeowner's impressive collection of natural wicker Victorian furniture, which has a warm sepia tone, was

"I LIKE ROOMS THAT ADULTS, CHILDREN, AND FAMILY PETS

the starting point for the interior design scheme. "We placed the pieces throughout the house and used a palette of taupe and rose shades against walls that are a wonderful clotted-cream color," Perlini relates. "The colors look beautiful with the brown wicker. As the family uses the house year-round, the brown and rose colors give the rooms a warmth we wouldn't have gotten if we'd used typical white-and-blue summery colors."

In addition to their artful colors, Perlini rooms display a

CAN ALL SHARE."

A Chinese student desk works as a server for the Sheraton table and stenciled American East Coast chairs. The pond boat sailer is a working 19th-century pleasure craft. The Victorian chandelier, converted from gas, illuminates the seaside dining room. **Opposite:** An early American Empire sideboard stores china and linens.

Perlini mixes fine reproductions, such as this copy of an Anglo-Indian bed, with antique side tables, such as this Victorian wicker. **Opposite:** An American mahogany Empire chest with classic column details and a marble top provides extra bath storage. Hanging etched lights are 19th-century American.

"I LIKE A VARIETY OF FURNITURE SHAPES AND FORMS, SOME BIGGER, OTHERS SMALLER."

In a guest room of classic American antiques, walnut canopy beds mix with natural wicker, Victorian side chairs, and an early-19th-century washstand. The clock is in the steeple style of the Gothic Revival period that followed the Civil War.

In this living room, an unusual 19th-century Boston looking-glass clock hangs above an American Hepplewhite chest of drawers. A new use for an antique, the handy drink table is a former 19th-century candle stand. **Opposite:** A gilded and lacquered Oriental table gives weight to an airy room, and displays a footed tole dish from France and a 19th-century etched-glass lantern. The bamboo chair is American Victorian.

liveliness that comes from her own sense of whimsy. Often, she employs painted decoration to achieve witty effects. "If someone has a plain wooden floor, I might suggest doing a painted-inlay pattern in several wood-tone stains," she explains. "It creates a trompe l'oeil parquet design and turns a floor that's not very exciting into something unique and rich." In a lighthearted turn, a sisal rug, with a painted design taken from a Sultanbad Persian

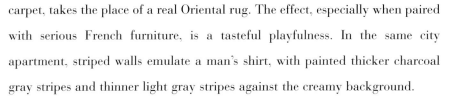

"I USED A PALETTE OF TAUPE AND ROSE SHADES AGAINST WALLS THAT ARE A CLOTTED-CREAM."

carpet, takes the place of a real Oriental rug. The effect, especially when paired with serious French furniture, is a tasteful playfulness. In the same city apartment, striped walls emulate a man's shirt, with painted thicker charcoal gray stripes and thinner light gray stripes against the creamy background.

The environments Perlini designs have polished manners, yet they are remarkably welcoming and comfortable. A living room can easily be the back-drop for a glittery formal cocktail party one evening and, on the morning after, become a comfortable family sanctuary for relaxing amid scattered newspapers and a snoozing Labrador retriever. "I like rooms that adults, children, and family pets can all share," she says. "That's a simple way to sum up my work."

129

Opposite: In the eclectic spirit of a 19th-century sea captain's house, an American bamboo cabinet mixes with a French farm table. The upholstered banquette is Perlini's relaxed contemporary touch. **Above:** Old and new meld seamlessly in the new country kitchen, where antique glass light fixtures illuminate the granite-clad island. Beadboard and brass drawer pulls contribute to the warm ambience. **Above right:** Cupboards with plain-style glass doors and backed with ivy wallpaper add decorative interest to the kitchen's work area. Butcher block offers a durable surface and the warmth of natural wood. **Right:** A knife box on a stand elevates an ornate Victorian-era silver clock; the burnt bamboo chair, popular in the 19th century, mixes with a collection of wicker from the exuberant design period. Perlini designs traditional-style upholstered pieces for contemporary comfort.

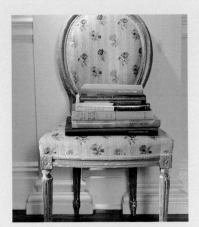

Well versed in European and American antiques, Paula Perlini has a special fondness for the infinite styles of accent chairs. Unlike case goods or larger upholstered pieces, smaller antique chairs are easy to move, arrange, add, or subtract at will or whim. Chairs favored by Perlini and her clients range from the unusual—the Italian voyeur chair in silk, **opposite**—to such classics as the sleek Louis XVI-style side chair, **above center,** to the stenciled American side chairs **above right** and **below right.** On a somewhat grander scale, the scrolled-arm, early-19th-century neoclassic armchair, upholstered in leather, **above left,** reflects strong forms and Greek inspirations. By the mid and late 19th century, the Victorian period infused furniture and decorative arts with particularly exuberant styles and motifs and exotic materials, **lower center.** The painted wicker corner chair, **below left,** features the Prince of Wales feathers motif, popular at the zenith of the British Empire.

CHAIRS of every size, shape, and style

CONFIDE
WITH
COLOR

WITH KELLY

Color is king when it comes to creating

NCE

memorable rooms. A sure hand with this

magical force can imbue interiors with any

wished-for mood, from dramatic to demure,

romantic to rocking. Sure is one of the many

A M E N

talents of Kelly Amen, a maestro at

Kelly Amen

orchestrating color (as well as design's

other tools) for ultimate pleasure and impact.

I nterior design begins with color and the reflection of light from that color," says Houston, Texas, interior designer Kelly Amen. His shimmering hues, exotic glazes, and daringly tinted ceilings create sophisticated backdrops for family antiques, fine contemporary art, and his own custom-designed furnishings.

"For me, the excitement comes from working with sur-

"COLOR GIVES YOU THE ABILITY NOT TO RUSH INTO THE POSSESSION OF OBJECTS."

prising and playful hues that represent an unusual juxtaposition," Amen continues. "If you stick with the laws of nature—light, the colors of the earth—rather than someone else's rules, you can never go wrong." In Amen-designed environments, walls are layered with greens suggesting a shadowy forest, or textured with a melding of plum and lavender to pay homage to the passing of the seasons. Pearl tints glaze gold ceilings, and amber and ivory washes heighten the drama of aubergine.

"I can't say exactly why such combinations work," Amen says. "I see and feel colors and the energy they create together." This seeing and feeling, along with an independent spirit, has its roots in Amen's Oklahoma childhood and artistic talents. "I can't remember when I wasn't arranging and rearranging," Amen recalls. "My mother tells the story of how I first started moving her flower vases around when I was a small child. I never stopped."

With such an early interest in decorating and art, Amen studied interior design at the University of Oklahoma and made the deliberate choice to work for an upscale Houston department store. "I chose not to work for an independent designer because I didn't want to be influenced by someone else's viewpoint," he says. By 1974, he had established his

Amen designed the foyer and adjoining dining room walls and ceilings as studies in reflected colors and light. The hand-painted border, in warm, rusty shades, alludes to ancient frescoes, and walls are decoratively painted with tints of sand and terra-cotta. The gold-leaf mirror hangs over one of the designer's signature mirrored walls. Taffeta silk draperies recall swirling ball gowns.

own design studio, with clients who appreciated his penchant for bold color and experimentation. Amen's free design spirit has been balanced with an educated eye for art and fine antiques. "One of the most interesting aspects of design is that I don't have the reverence that can stifle so much of the creative process," he explains.

"I've never had anyone tell me I couldn't, shouldn't, or might not." Instead, Amen works with clients as he refines the interchange of color and texture and the deft mix of traditional versus contemporary that are his career constants. The stunning, striking results are sometimes serious, sometimes whimsically flirtatious.

"The stimulation of design is there will always be surprises in any project," he adds. "The best elements of design to my mind are the beautiful mistakes that just happen and are exactly right. The process is one of boldly jumping in and going where the project leads you."

For Amen, the process begins with color in ever-changing hues, tints, and techniques. "Color is life to me; color inspires me. Once my clients live with color, they find it almost impossible to live without it. Taking that first bold step can be very unnerving, but painting a room is the least expensive thing you can do. And the more layers you put on, the more luxurious it becomes. People worry too

much about matching colors in design. I don't think you can ever match—light and sun are always changing—but you can successfully blend or massage colors."

What Amen does exceptionally well is create whole-house color schemes for his clients. Sometimes, he works totally from scratch; other times he starts with clients' rugs, art, or upholstered furniture. "For every house I do, I begin with about two hundred colors I put on a table, and I pick from there," the designer explains. "I find I need that many for the choices I want." From the palettes of several favorite paint companies, Amen edits down to about 70 choices, then to about 30 favored shades for the custom finishes he tends to use in most of his projects.

"Then I walk through the house and start my placement on the walls and ceilings," he explains. "I'm open to what will work. Color gives you the ability to not hurry into the possession of objects. When a home is beautifully painted and the shell is beautiful, you can take your time to find the right furniture and art."

Just as he doesn't limit himself to numbers of colors, neither does Amen impose restrictions on paint finishes or decorative treatments. "One of the things I most like to do with a color is to choose one wonderful, rich dramatic shade and then have it applied in matte, eggshell, gloss,

Opposite: Daring color, a self-portrait by Kermit Oliver, and antiques combine in creative synergy for the foyer and dining room. Seafoam green walls, highlighted with taupe and gold, coolly frame an opulent room designed for entertaining. **Above:** A hanging light fixture works as contemporary art against the mottled green walls of an upstairs landing.

Amen intensifies colors by choosing dramatic shades and faux finishes for adjoining rooms. Lavender walls, laced with plum, play off the aubergine of the music room's ceiling. Armchairs with an ottoman replace the more conventional sofa and coffee table.

and glaze finishes in the same room—from walls and built-ins to the ceiling and trim. The mix always seems incredible as light hits the finishes from different vantage points."

Coloring the ceiling is an Amen signature of which he is justly proud. "The ceiling is one-sixth of the space of a room," he says. "To me, it's criminal to leave it unappointed. I go beyond doing a tint of the wall color to choosing a color and a glaze that are beautiful in their own right."

"THE CEILING IS ONE-SIXTH OF THE SPACE OF A ROOM; IT'S CRIMINAL

With so much saturated color in a room, the designer finds visual relief in the trims. "The crispness and contrast of the woodwork against layers of paint on the wall and ceiling are always interesting," he continues. "I enjoy the effect of painting all the woodwork in a house either white or a neutral and glazing it either ecru or beige. The consistency of the woodwork throughout the house is one of those design quirks that I find stimulating. It's a unifying technique."

Also unifying is Amen's use of mirrors—as wall treatment, backdrops for built-ins, or beautifully framed art. "Mirroring is fabulous because people become the art," the designer says. "Mirrored surfaces help you do something wonderful in transitional spaces such as foyers or halls. I enjoy the effect of art or a framed mirror hung over a mirrored wall. And one of my favorite ways is to leave a window undressed or barely dressed and double the light with

Right: Amen designed the stone-top bronze bench as the first piece in his furniture collection. **Opposite top:** This "chair brassiere," a clipped-corner fabric cover for the piano seat, allows peeks of the burled wood. **Opposite:** In a library warmed by textures, a kilim rug covers a vintage armchair with carved detailing and nailheads.

TO LEAVE IT UNAPPOINTED."

The entry makes a strong design statement with the faux-finished green walls and terracotta ceiling as backdrop for an Amen-designed aluminum console table with sandstone top. **Opposite:** Bedroom walls and ceiling quieten the mood with shades of buff and umber. Amen designed the upholstered bed.

"I ENCOURAGE MY CLIENTS TOWARD
A MINIMALISM WITH THEIR ACCESSORIES."

a mirrored wall that accents windows or window seats."

From these backdrops, which he calls the shells of interiors, Amen moves seamlessly to the furnishings. He often works with family antiques, frequently pairing them with his own custom-designed pieces. And with his interest in art, he uses Houston artists to create painted designs of flowers, animals, and even insects for silk chair or sofa coverings. "This is a great way to cover those inevitable spots on upholstery when a family lives in their house," he says. "I like something a client once said: 'The trace of human beings has never been alarming to me.'"

Recycling is another of Amen's talents. He encourages clients to save old draperies or upholstery that can be recycled for sofa or floor pillows. "Elements of our past lives should be carried into each new transition as our lives change and we adjust to new situations," he adds.

But what the designer calls integration of the old and new, past and present, also means careful refinement of elements. "I encourage my clients toward a minimalism with their accessories. Filling bookshelves with books you don't read or cluttering the coffee table with five hundred things is frankly a nuisance. And who wants to bother with that much inventory in life? Besides, if you pick only the best, or pick what you love to live with every day, you can integrate any period or style into your home. That's a Kelly Amen rule. And I don't make many rules."

Although he helps clients choose art and accessories with discernment, a Kelly Amen-designed home isn't truly finished. "Interior design is an evolution," he says. "It never stops. When you quit adding one little element of change, a room dies. A room should be like a beautiful, classic dress that you keep changing with your accessories."

Amen worked with Houston artist Theo Ostler to create the fantasy wall finish that cools the brilliance of the circa-1920 Chinese rug. Enriching the mix are the Venetian glass mirror and the custom-made poufed and fringed cat bed.

 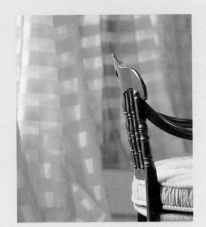 

Traditional fabrics and finishes pair with contemporary pieces, and contemporary textiles update the most traditional of fine furnishings in Kelly Amen-designed rooms. In projects where using the finest-quality materials and craftsmanship is the only abiding rule, Amen's careful eye is the final arbiter of what colors, fabrics, textiles, and details interact to best advantage. Window treatments range from voluminous yards of silk and taffeta paired with rich damasks, **opposite** and **above center,** to barely-there, light-softening designs. Textures, too, enhance his schemes with the play of kilim rugs as fabrics, **below left,** to the richly trimmed velvets on the chair, **below right,** to his own custom table of metal and stone, **below center.** As a signature touch, Amen commissions artists to paint details on fabrics that produce one-of-a-kind pieces, **above left.** He advocates recycling clients' fabrics into detailed, well-dressed pillows when styles of rooms and color schemes change.

Updating traditional with contemporary TEXTURE

CULTUR

CROSSROADS

WITH DOUG

Interior design that reflects the multitude of

global influences in today's world can

heighten the joy of everyday living. A

Doug Rasar

home that combines multicultural elements can be

the ultimate expression of universal beauty

AL

and serenity. Long a melting pot of cultures,

philosophies, and arts, the Pacific Northwest

has a master of holistic design in Doug Rasar.

RASAR

The decorative legacies of Europe and Asia, architectural prints and garden design, serenely neutral backdrops and richly saturated colors—these are all part of the refined mix of current interior design. But the core of what makes a pleasing home extends beyond choosing and arranging beautiful objects in equally beautiful spaces. Thoughtful design considers the architectural context in which objects are placed, the nuances of lighting, and the relationship of the house to its setting.

Seattle interior designer Doug Rasar is a strong proponent of this "holistic" approach to design. "Home is the primary place where people seek sanctuary from their hectic lives and spend any amount of quality time," he says. "It is a bit of a sacred trust to work on someone's home and create a place where it's possible to relax, recharge, and fill in the gaps of one's life. Mere decoration isn't enough."

Rasar's talent for creating quiet and order amidst chaotic life comes partially from where he lives and works—on the edge of the Pacific Rim. "Although my first love is classical European design, I've also been greatly influenced by the beauty of the Orient—especially the concept of home as a place for peaceful contemplation," he says. He was also influenced by his long stint as an interior designer for a Seattle architecture firm. "I know that working as part of a full design team of architects, lighting experts, and landscape architects has affected my work," he says. "I learned to think in terms of the entire picture, not just me."

With this background, Rasar started his own design firm in 1994, but he still puts great stock in the team approach. "Most of my projects involve new houses or major remodelings, so I almost always work with an architect."

Because he strongly believes in design tailored to each client's needs, interests, and family histories, Rasar discusses his philosophy in terms of consistent elements and recurring themes, rather than specific styles or periods. "I always break a room down into three simplified areas— the shell, the major furnishing pieces, and the art and accessories. If one is missing, the room never seems complete, no matter how fine the other two elements are," he explains.

In executing his comprehensive design approach, Rasar always begins his projects with the creation of a beautiful shell. "I don't decorate; that's not what clients hire me to do," he says. Instead, he takes cues from detailing, finishing materials, and architectural and decorative lighting. "Every project is different because every client is different, though that sounds like a cliché. But there are themes in

Opposite: Doug Rasar copied an antique ball-and-claw-foot Chippendale side chair to create a set of six. The iron-and-glass lantern is a reproduction; the rug is a custom design. **Above:** Grouped collections seem more important than scattered pieces. An English breakfront displays Rose Medallion porcelains. The bowl is also Rose Medallion.

In this sunroom-as-living-room, the stone tiles and tabletop urn recall grand conservatories, while the lushly upholstered furniture gives comfort with a hint of formality. The hand-painted cornice; whimsical, painted ottoman; and bronze caryatids (female-form columns) enrich the personal mix.

The repetition of red, from the Herez living room rug to the silk-clad library walls to tabletop accessories, visually strengthens the spaces. The abstract above the piano, by Spanish painter Joan Miró, repeats the simplicity of the Oriental pieces. **Below right:** Checkerboard fabric relaxes the pair of armchairs in the formal library.

my work that keep repeating. For example, I particularly like rooms that have a connection to the gardens, and I strive for the inside-outside relationship whenever possible," he says. "I like the effect of using garden elements inside."

Rasar is drawn to neutrals, most often off-whites and greiges (beige and gray mixes) or to rich, saturated hues such as red tinged with orange and small

"WE FIND THE ASIAN SENSIBILITIES WORK VERY WELL WITH MODERN FURNITURE PIECES."

touches of black. Occasionally, depending on client preference, he includes fabric-covered walls as part of the mix. The designer takes advantage of his architectural background to incorporate classical motifs in stenciled oak floors or inlaid stone. While he likes the contrast of dark-stained wood floors with off-white or greige, he also employs natural, unstained maple in light-hued rooms.

Whatever the mix of walls and floor surfaces, lighting is the element that brings the shell to life. "From the inception of a project, I work with the architect on the architectural lighting plan, as I know the major furniture and art and their placements," Rasar says. "Then we turn the plan over to a lighting

Opposite: In a study of East meets West, a contemporary silk Fortuny shade from Italy illuminates the vaulted, custom-lacquered foyer ceiling and the carved Chinese altar table. The lamps were originally Chinese candlesticks. Rasar designed the floor's geometric stenciled motifs. **Left:** This rare 1740s Italian chest is noteworthy for the detailed inlay of a classical architectural perspective; the top is the original marble. French Empire lamps feature the griffin motif commonly used in the 19th century. The mirror is a 19th-century French antique, and the mahogany chair is 18th-century English. **Above right:** White marble clads the top of the 1820s Karl Johnna gilt console from Sweden. The mirror is gilt wood from the Italian Baroque period (circa 1720s). **Above left:** Etchings from the owners' collection hang in a grid pattern above a bleached rosewood English game table with a lyre base (circa 1820s).

"I LIKE THE IDEA OF ANTIQUES THAT PROVIDE A CONNECTION FOR CLIENTS AND THEIR PASTS."

Red walls contrast beautifully with the hand-gilded, ornate antique French iron bed dressed in contemporary linens. **Opposite:** The gilded French-style chair is a rare and collectible reproduction crafted in Egypt in the 1920s. An antique incense burner and antique botanical prints dress the mantel.

Fabric in the Arts and Crafts style creates the decorative cornice below the original coffered-beamed ceiling of this Seattle Craftsman-style house. Rasar designed the fireplace tile surround in appropriate style; the fire screen is original. **Opposite:** Beaded shades dress the antique crystal chandelier.

Irish ancestry, for example, I help them find some Irish antiques." For notes of formality, Rasar introduces French and Italian pieces, particularly in styles with references to Greek or Roman classicism. "And there's also a romanticism to French and Italian that appeals to me," he notes. Asian pieces are likely, too, to surface in the mix. "Many of my clients are collectors because of business or travel," he says. "We find the Asian sensibilities combine very well with modern furniture pieces. Accents range from tables and screens to porcelains and art."

Rasar says his love of the garden and garden elements, as well as simple window treatments, are reflections of the melding of East and West. "I enjoy garden ornaments brought indoors, such as gazing balls and old finials, and I like spaces with large windows and low sills where the lines blur between indoors and outdoors. There's a serenity to the garden that's very Eastern," he says. In the spirit of the Eastern garden, Rasar says he also frequently uses bamboo

shades, or if privacy isn't an issue, he leaves windows uncovered. When rooms call for formal treatments, he designs fixed panels, often silk, with exposed rods and custom finials. In other settings, he favors well-detailed

"FROM THE INCEPTION OF A PROJECT, I WORK WITH THE ARCHITECT

Roman or French balloon shades. "Details are everything. Their presence, especially as related to fabric treatments, separates a professional from a do-it-yourselfer," he says.

This refined art of the mix is equally evident in Rasar's carefully edited choices of art and accessories. Depending on the project, the designer may use a large contemporary painting, a family piece, or fine Asian porcelains, such as Rose Medallion. He is also partial to very old botanical prints and Piranesi etchings from the 1700s. "Here again, it's the garden and architectural interest," he says. When it comes to floor coverings, the designer has several favorites—antique tribal rugs, French Aubusson carpets, and custom-woven raffia rugs, which are a cut above sisal.

No matter how serene the surroundings or sublime the architectural and decorative appointments, a room isn't complete, Rasar says. "A room isn't finished until it has what I call 'the little things that are magic'—curtains wafting or billowing in the breeze, flickering candles, dancing sunlight, mirrors across from mirrors reflecting infinity. In the end, those are the touches that make a beautiful room."

Right: Glass walls with views of downtown Seattle flank a decorative bracket with an Indonesian mask. Rasar designed the glass coffee table and gently curved sofas. **Opposite top:** A beautifully executed kitchen opens into the dining room where the skyline is art. **Opposite bottom:** The burled ash Charles X (circa 1830s) library table anchors the open dining area.

ON THE LIGHTING PLAN."

In the East-meets-West environment of the Pacific Northwest, designer Doug Rasar works with design motifs and finishing touches that incorporate diverse histories and cultures. In this cosmopolitan milieu, he finds inspiration from the Orient in the homes and collections of his well-traveled clients. Ornately carved, intricately detailed Chinese tables, **below center** and **below right,** are treasured pieces that work beautifully in lively family homes. Rasar also finds design renewal in Arts and Crafts architecture, which turned to the Medieval period as a balance to excesses of the early 20th century. In an Arts and Crafts-era home, he lightened the stairwell trim for the contrast of shapes and pattern, **below left**. And in the same home, he introduced pillows of rich velvet, **above right,** that allude to the mythical images of the Middle Ages. As relief from touches of the opulent, Rasar turns to simplified neoclassic motifs, such as the sink, **above left,** and the plates, **above center**.

ANCIENT patterns make timeless rooms

Geometry is a recurring motif in Rasar's intellectual, architecturally influenced designs. Recalling the inspirations of ancient cultures, from the Egyptians to the Chinese to the Persians and Greeks, his designs include mosaics of the circles of life and twining vines, **above left**. For an intricately stenciled and stained floor, Rasar included the classic motifs of diamond, circle, and star, **above center,** that transcend periods and cultures. In a further play on geometry and symbols, a door design features the cross design of inter-locking lines with a decorative center medallion, **above right**. And in geometry that recalls both the Middle Ages and contemporary art, tile rectangles and diamonds decorate the fireplace surround and hearth, **below right**. Furnishings and fabric, too, illustrate the geometric forms, as in a rare antique inlaid Italian chest, **below left,** and the stylized, straight lines of the tailored window valance and centered lantern fixture, **below center**.

Creating a backdrop using geometric SHAPES

ACHIEVING
TIMELE
EASE

WITH ALESSANDRA

Trendy is the last word in Alessandra Branca's

SS multilingual vocabulary. And the designer would

like you to adopt the same practice. Interiors born

of this appreciation for timeless good taste need

little getting used to—you just immediately fall in love

BRANCA

with their understated style. Branca's

Alessandra Branca

interiors have a relaxed elegance that verges

on being wholesome. Your mom would approve.

When your grandfather was an art historian and art critic for the Vatican newspapers, your view of history and its design lessons might be somewhat longer term than most. "Having grown up in a city that's two thousand years old made a huge difference in the way I view things," says the Italian-born, Chicago-based interior designer Alessandra Branca. "I tell clients a home comes together slowly, in layers. It is easily a two- to three-year process, and we try to make it enjoyable for them. A great

"HAVE SOMETHING GILDED AND SOMETHING DISTRESSED TO ADD AGE."

antique ages with patina over time, and the same process will make your home warm and beautiful. It takes care and love and time. Design isn't an overnight project."

Branca came to the world of interior design from another related field—fine art. After finishing college in the United States, she opened a gallery devoted to antique prints, a passion since she was 14 years old. "The gallery was like a living room with comfortable sofas and chairs," Branca recalls. "A client loved the feel of the space and asked if I could do something like it for him. We ended up doing four homes together."

This early success solidified Branca's design direction of combining classic shapes, forms, and details into rooms clearly planned for contemporary family living. "I design for who someone is now and where they are going in the future," say Branca, who lives in a 19th-century

Branca chooses classic furniture forms, arranged symmetrically, for her living room. Boldly striped fabric on the Louis XVI chairs and at the windows provides contemporary balance. The Louis XVI console, under the watercolor, displays a bouilotte lamp.

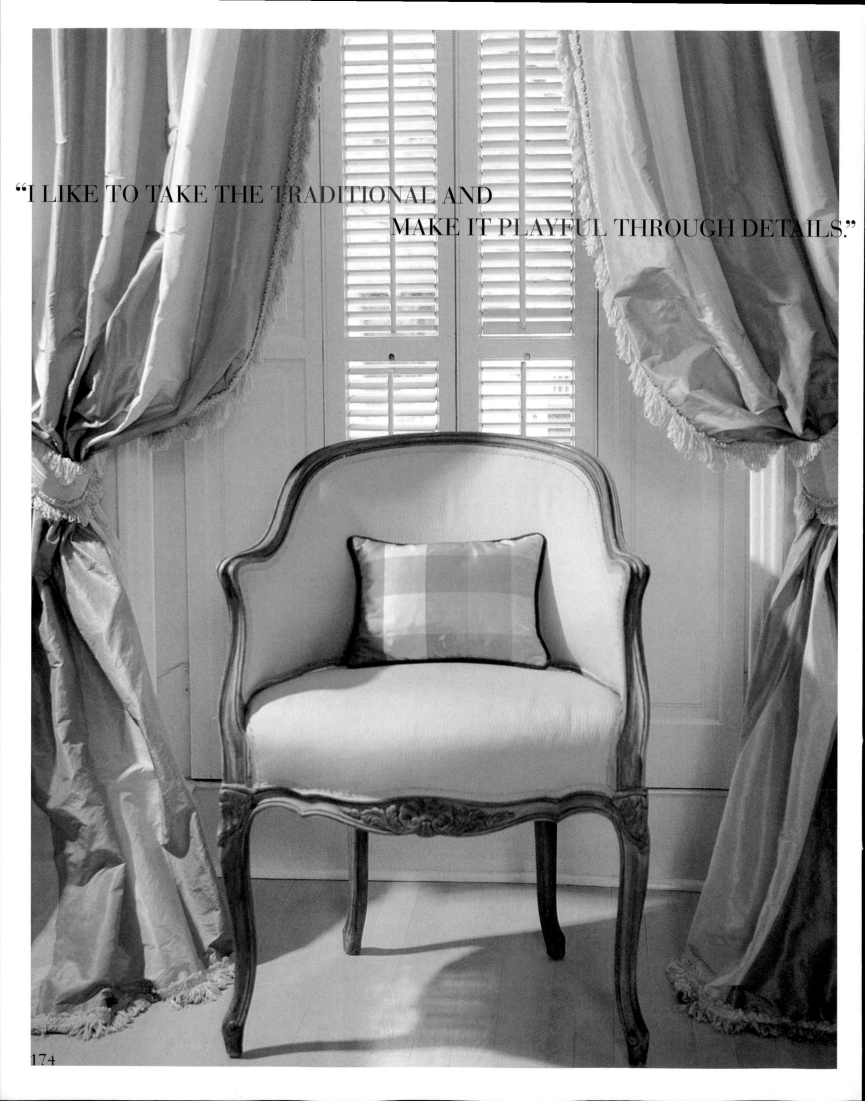

"I LIKE TO TAKE THE TRADITIONAL AND MAKE IT PLAYFUL THROUGH DETAILS."

In a foyer, a tailored banded sisal rug gives youthful balance to the formal gilt chinoiserie mirror hung above the Louis XIV-style demilune console, which was painted in Branca's studio. The bench is in the English Georgian style. **Opposite:** Taffeta draperies frame a Louis XV chair in front of shutters original to the late-19th-century city house.

townhouse with her husband and three children. "For me, a home is always a work in progress."

In order to build such flexibility into a design scheme, Branca approaches each project with a strategic plan. "We sit down with the client and ask them what they want and where do they think they are going to be in five years," she says. "We want the home to grow and evolve so that it's better in ten years, not outdated in two."

Branca also catalogs the furnishings her clients already own, helping them assess their collection and giving them ideas on what to purchase. "We take a photographic inventory of all furniture, paintings, and accessories, and put it in a book, along with the dimensions of each piece," she explains. "We do a floor plan of the room in two ways, one showing it connect-

ed to the other rooms, the other showing the space alone. Then we start assigning the furniture they own to each room, and I propose additional pieces we could fill in. Rarely do we throw things away."

Branca's facility in devising practical, multipurpose solutions within spaces that are beautiful is one of her most outstanding skills. Interestingly enough, the idea mirrors the interior schemes of the 18th and early 19th centuries, when rooms, even in large houses, served a number of pur-

poses. A Branca-designed dining room, for example, may have grand moldings and billowing silk curtains, but it will be furnished with cushiony upholstery and a retractable table so that it can function as a second living room. And in a living room, she may include a desk, a game table, and an elegant painted armoire to conceal a television, elements that allow the room to serve many comfortable uses.

"I don't like a space that ties you down," the designer explains. "I like a room that is flexible and gives you options. For example, when I design a family room, I plan it for all the things you would do. I'll include a dining area, a desk, a couple of club chairs, a comfortable wing chair where you can read, and a big center table with books and magazines."

By adapting old ideas to new situations, Branca creates the timeless looks she advocates. Leather is used mainly for upholstery in America, but in Europe, leather has appeared since the Renaissance as decorative elements on a variety of surfaces. "I designed a leather library floor in a herringbone pattern for a client's loft, which was the raw space of an abandoned cookie factory we converted," Branca says. "We used padded leather doors with nailheads to soundproof and divide the space. And we did leather binding on the carpet. Those are the kind of traditional details I use to give a twist to a room."

Red walls and the generously sized dining table balance the grand architecture of the dining room. *The Enfanta* by Velásquez inspired the design of the fire screen, painted by Branca's mother, Anna Chiara Branca, who also painted the watercolors.

Unexpected details on the upholstery are another signature of Branca's style. She may wrap a club chair in two contrasting fabrics, or she may embellish the backrest of a Directoire armchair with a cutout appliqué. "I often refer to costume books. The details of clothing intrigue me—the covered bows on 18th-century dresses or the way 1920s and 1930s clothing looks," she says. "I might put a

"I LIKE A ROOM THAT IS FLEXIBLE AND GIVES YOU OPTIONS."

vent on the back of a chair skirt and line the inside of it with a contrasting fabric. We often trim chairs in custom gimps and use leather, silver, or gold custom nailheads."

Such attention to detail pulls Branca's rooms together, creating unique personal spaces that reflect the client's personality. Hand-painted, one-of-a-kind furniture and accessories, fabricated in Branca's studio, lend an artisan-crafted uniqueness to all her environments. Her mother, Anna Chiara Branca, is a talented artist who creates some of these striking pieces. "A gilded or faux-bois mirror, a painted lamp, a japanned desk—such pieces customize a room and give it a patina," Branca says .

As the project develops, Branca's signature touches emerge. The upholstery will be custom-made, the fabrics will be European, the window treatments will be generously scaled to complement the proportions and moldings of windows. Walls will probably be solid color rather than

Right: Branca designed the bed in the lavish style of the 18th century with damask curtains and custom-made trims, including the rosette. **Opposite top:** Striped walls and a checkered fabric infuse the bedroom with lively style. **Opposite bottom:** In a living room of refined color, pattern, and 18th-century decorative arts, the gilded bench is French while the antique sconce is English.

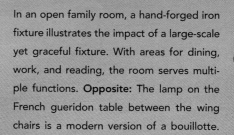

In an open family room, a hand-forged iron fixture illustrates the impact of a large-scale yet graceful fixture. With areas for dining, work, and reading, the room serves multiple functions. **Opposite:** The lamp on the French gueridon table between the wing chairs is a modern version of a bouillotte.

THEY GROUND A ROOM."

patterned. "I do think people and art are better displayed if the backgrounds are not patterned," the designer notes. "I like to include a few black accents because it grounds a room and gives it strength. I think it is good to have something gilded and something distressed in a room to add some age. I don't specifically go out and use these rules for every job I do. These are just aspects of my style."

Because Branca considers design an educational process, she devotes time to opening up possibilities for her clients. "We introduce them to furniture styles they may not have thought of—Continental antiques, Swedish, Dutch, Italian," she says. "They may not be as familiar with these as they are with English and French furnishings."

But the designer firmly advises not succumbing to a style for style's sake. "The minute something looks like it's a trend, I avoid it," she says. "If you get locked into a trendy style, it may have passed before you have finished your home." Spoken like a true believer in the long-term view.

Below: For a family room, Branca designed an ottoman with a pullout tray for snacks and metal accent tables created for the space. The metal repeats in the wire-clad cabinet doors. **Left:** The custom sofa, refined from a 1920s design, features sturdy quilted fabric and nailhead trim. **Far left:** A custom stone base pairs with Directoire-style chairs.

Above: An early-19th-century rug sets the color scheme for a room with reproduction French fabrics. **Right:** This Directoire chair takes on a spirited attitude with new oversize plaid updated with a cutout from reproduction French antique fabric. **Far right:** A tole lamp from the Paris flea market graces a Louis XVI-style desk made by a Parisian firm.

Branca starts her projects with a sure understanding of classic furniture pieces, custom craftsmanship, and fine, usually European, fabrics. In a bedroom for young brothers, **opposite,** she designed a pair of trundle beds with tailored, piped upholstered headboards. The red, black, and white fabric scheme is lively without seeming juvenile. The gentle curve of the Directoire-style chair, **above left,** plays off against the bold stripes of the banquette. Branca finds inspiration in the strong shapes of postwar furniture. She re-covered the armless '50s chair, **above center,** and trimmed it with tape and nailheads. The French-style chair with bolster, **above right,** and the 1930s-inspired chairs with curvy, exaggerated shapes, **below right,** are freshened with a light, checked fabric. Her penchant for shapes extends to the wavy mantel, **below center.** A sleigh-back chair, **below left,** takes on contemporary flair with a mix of a print and tailored plaid, finished with twill tape and nailheads.

Furniture is less serious, more WHIMSICAL

SOURCES

TRANSCONTINENTAL FRENCH STYLE
PAGE 14

Interior design—Charles Faudree, Charles Faudree, Inc., 1345 E. 15th St.,Tulsa, OK 74120; 918/747-9706.

Pages 16-23 (living room): Fabric for sofa (Curzon Check), drapery trim (Oleander Tassel)—Brunschwig & Fils; 212/838-7878. Fabric for sofa pillows, chair cushion, and draperies (La Bussiere)—Pierre Frey; 212/213-3099. Bennison fabric for pillow (Rose); Marvic fabric for chairs (Les Enfants)—George Cameron Nash; 214/744-1544.

Pages 24-25 (kitchen): Wallpaper (Oakley)—Brunschwig & Fils; 212/838-7878. Cabinets—Master's Custom Woodworks; 918/663-5870. Fabric for cupboard (La Buissere)—Pierre Frey; 212/213-3099.

Pages 26-27 (lower left photo): Wallpaper (La Chasse II)—Decorator's Walk; 713/629-6340. Dining room: Fabric for draperies (Grilly cotton), drapery trim (Oleander Tassel)—Brunschwig & Fils; 212/838-7878. Fabric for antique chairs (Mederbes)—Pierre Frey; 212/213-3099.

Pages 28-29 (library): Fabric for draperies (Potomac linen), fabric for sofa (On Point cotton)—Brunschwig & Fils; 212/838-7878. Trim (Natural)—Payne Fabrics, Inc.; 800/543-4322. Fabric for wing chairs (Halte De Chasse)—Pierre Frey; 212/213-3099. Marvic fabric for sofa pillows (Les Muses et Le Leon)—George Cameron Nash; 214/744-1544. Carpet (Leopard)—Stanton Carpet; 516/822-5878. Needlepoint pillow —Vaughn Designs; 212/319-7070.

Pages 30-31 (formal dining room): Wallpaper (La Chasse II)—Decorator's Walk; 713/629-6340. Fabric for chairs—Brunschwig & Fils; 212/838-7878.

Pages 32-34 (bedroom): Fabric for wing chair and draperies (Le Meunier et Fils), wallpaper (Band Royale)—F. Schumacher & Co.; 800/332-3384.

Page 35 (master bathroom): Fabric for chair and walls (Le Meunier et Fils)—Schumacher; 800/332-3384. Rug—Stanton Carpet; 516/822-5878. Bathroom: Zoffany wallpaper (Pavilion)—Whittaker & Woods; 770/438-8760.

TWIST ON TRADITION
PAGE 38

Interior design—Mary Douglas Drysdale, Drysdale Design Associates, 1733 Connecticut Ave., NW, Washington, DC 20009; 202/588-0700.

Page 41 (entry): Morgan center table—Dessin-Fournir; 626/856-1768. Fabric for draperies (Trianon Printed Ceci #C2-301-2P)—Christopher Norman; 212/644-4100. Drapery trim (RTF-84204)—Rogers Textiles & Trims; 773/745-6577. Rug (Abaca wool)—Surface Mills; 310/276-5252. Fabric for chair and pillows (Limoges silk)—Scalamandré; 212/980-3888. Antique weather vane, millwork, and neoclassical side chairs—Drydale Design.

Pages42-45 (living room): A. Rudin sofas—Profiles; 212/689-6903. Fabric for sofas and draperies (Portofino #087, draperies include Gauffrage #4332)—Manuel Canovas; 212/752-9588. Pollack & Associates fabric for window sheers (Crosscurrent #9016/01)—Donghia; 212/935-3713. neoclassical armchairs (Italian)—Florian Papp; 212/288-6770. Fabric for armchairs and pillows (Fleury #82)—Nobilis; 908/464-1177. Louis XVI-style occasional tables and Nubien Régence sconce—Christopher Norman; 212/644-4100. Rug (Belvedere-Balfour)—Hokanson; 713/621-6609. Living room, through columns: Louis XV-style lounge chairs and ottomans—Holly Hunt New York; 212/755-6555. Fabric for Louis XV-style lounge chairs, ottomans, and draperies (Portofino #087, draperies include Gauffrage #4332)—Manuel Canovas; 212/752-9588. Jagtar fabric for chair backs (Directoire Stripe)—Kirk Brummel

Showroom; 202/646-1664. Fabric for draperies (St. Tropez Stripe), fabric for sheers (Summer Snow)—J. Robert Scott; 310/659-4910. Drapery banding (La Fenice)—Bergamo Fabrics, Inc.; 212/462-1010. Merida rug (Foundation-Straw)—J. Brooks Designer Floors; 703/698-0790.

Pages 46-47 (dining room): Furniture and art—Drysdale Design

Pages 50-51 (library): Sofa (Studded Shelter)—Saladino Funiture, Inc.; 212/838-0500. Leather—Dualoy Leather, Inc.; 212/736-3360. Fabric for pillows—(Patola Stripe) Osborne & Little; 212/751-3333. Fabric for pillows (Brantome wool)—Manuel Canovas; 212/752-9588. Fabric for bolster pillow (Carmen)—Old World Weavers; 212/355-7186. Chairs —Randolph & Hein; 415/864-3371. Zimmer & Rohde fabric for chairs (Ossian #1904-2170)—Holly Hunt New York: 212/755-6555. Rodolph fabric for shade (Heir Apparent #HA6105A)—Donghia; 212/935-3713. Sisal (Presley Natural)—Stark Carpet; 212/752-9000. Tables—Drysdale Design Associates. (Entry, lower right photo): settee—Drysdale Design; fabric (Diplomat)—Bergamo Fabric; 212/462-1010.

Pages 54-55 (breakfast room): Stenciled pedestal table and chairs—Drysdale Design. Jane Churchill fabric for seat (Armorial Trellis)—Cowtan & Tout; 212/753-4488. Fabric for window treatment (Pharoah's Stripe #1228)—J. Robert Scott; 310/659-4910. Fabric trim for window treatment—Rogers Textiles & Trims; 773/745-6577. Table, chair, and millwork—Drysdale Design. Den, lower right photo: Sofa—Saladino Furniture; 212/838-0500. Fabric for sofa (Tiburon solid chenille #131-84)—Myung Jin, Inc.; 415/331-6373. For pillow (Palazzo #491025)—Donghia; 212/935-3713. Sabre-leg table—Drysdale Design.

Pages 56-59 (bedroom): Carpet (Lorraine wool #5010)—Unique Carpets, Ltd. at Design Center Carpet; 202/6646-1300. Fabric for window treatments (Cambon Plaid silk #C2-601-07)—Christopher Norman; 212/644-4100. Louis XVI-style desk—Julia Grey Ltd.; 212/223-4454. Regina chair and armchair—J. Robert Scott; 310/659-4910. Fabric for chairs (Rainbow Velvet #98663-087)—Scalamandré; 212/980-3888. Victoria club chair and ottoman—Melrose House; 323/651-2202. Fabric for chair and ottoman (Mandor #4228/93)—Manuel Canovas; 212/752-9588. Fabric for duvet cover (Quintessence)—Phoenix Down Corp.; 973/812-8100. Fabric for settee (Portofino #4332/087)—Manuel Canovas; 212/752-9588. Bed, eettee, bench, console—Drysdale Design.

Page 58 (bathroom): Starburst mirror—Mirror Fair; 212/288-5050; Antique weather vane—Drysdale Design Associates; 202/588-0700.

UPDATING AMERICAN CLASSICS
PAGE 62

Interior design—Gary McBournie, Gary McBournie, Inc., 33 A N. Main St., Sherborn, MA 01770; 508/655-3887. Architects—Rafe & Priscilla Lowell, Architects, 20 N. Main Street, Sherborn, MA 01770; 508/655-4198; Stephen Judge and James Skelton, Judge, Skelton & Smith, Inc., 16 Joy St., Boston, MA 02114; 617/227-9062.

Pages 64-65, 67 (dining room): Windsor chairs, dining table, and three-seat bench—Spivack's Antiques. Quilt cushions—Rockport Quilt Shoppe. Braided rug—Stark Carpet; 212/752-9000. Dresser and sideboard—Pierre Deux Antiques, 369 Bleecker St., New York, NY 10014; 212/243-7740. Prints Roger Lussier, Inc., 168 Newbury St., Boston, MA 02116; 617/536-0069. Sconce, shade, and fabrication—Blanche P. Field. Bell jar—Treillage Ltd.; 212/535-2288. Trim (Tuxedo Park #PS101-0)—Carleton V; 718/706- 7780.

Fabrication—Strictly Decorative; 978/692-7760.

Page 66 (living room, upper right photo): Chair slipcover fabrication—Dilys Morris. Lamps—Blanche P. Field.

Pages 68-69 (living room): Twisted-led table—Spivack's Antiques. Lamp shade—Blanche P. Field. Framed needlepoint and boxes—Marcoz Antiques. Lounge chair—Hickory Chair Co.; 828/328-1801. Fabric for lounge chair (St. Tropez)—Orient Express; 800/776-6999. Fabric for pillow (#4233-25)—Manuel Canovas; 212/752-9588. Fabric trim for pillow (#891991)—F. Shumacher & Co.; 800/523-1200. Fabric welt for pillow (Miami)—Norbar Fabrics; 800/645-8501. Fabrication—Dilys Morris. Family room: Fabric for arm chair (Tuxedo Park #PS101-0)—Carleton V; 718/706-7780. Fabric trim for armchair (Nid d'Abeilles Braid #90016.05/209)—Brunschwig & Fils; 212/838-7878. Straight-arm sofa—Connors Design Ltd.; 508/429-4980. Fabric for straight-arm sofa and pillow (Kempton Check #JT10F-10)—Cowtan & Tout; 212/753-4488. Roll-arm sofa—Hickory Chair Co.; 828/328-1801. Fabric for front of lounge chair and sofa pillows (Windsor Rose #82000-1F)—Cowtan & Tout; 212/753-4488. Fabric for back (Miami)—Norbar Fabrics; 800/645-8501. Armchair, candlestick table, and lamp—John Rosselli International; 212/772-2137. Gourd vase lamp—John Boone, Inc.; 212/758-0012. Shade—Blanche P. Field. Trim for sheers (Tuxedo Park #PS101-0)—Carelton V; 718/706-7780. Fabrication—Strictly Decorative. Raffia table—Baker, Knapp & Tubbs; 312/329-9410. Candlesticks on trunk—Spivack's Antiques 781/235-1700. Quilt—Rockport Quilt Shoppe. Rug—Stark Carpet 212/752-9000.

Pages 70-71 (entry hall): Wallpaper (Strie #JS02W-08)—Cowtan & Tout; 212/753-4488. Antique ship modeló Nina Hellman Antiques, 48 Centre St., Nantucket, MA 02554; 508/228-4677. Star quilt—Rockport Quilt Shoppe. Tight-back sofa and chair—Connors Design Ltd.; 508/429-4980. Fabric for sofa (Tuxedo Park #PS101-0)—Carelton V; 718/706-7780. Fabric welt (Elite)—S. Harris Co.; 800/999-5600. Fabric for pillows (Orsini Check #103272)—Cowtan & Tout; 212/753-4488. Fabrication—Dilys Morris. Fabric for wingback (#62690.01)—Brunshwig & Fils; 212/838-7878. Coffee and side tables—Spivack's Antiques. Double-arm lamp (#27502DT)—McLean Lighting Works; 336/294-6994. Floor lamp—John Rosselli International; 212/772-2137. Shade—Blanche P. Field. Rug and runner (Seagrass)—Stark Carpet; 212/752-9000. Trim for rug and runner (#90054-184)—Brunschwig & Fils; 212/838-7878.

Page 73 (sitting room): Fabric for valance (Tuxedo Park PS101-0)—Carlton V; 718/706-7780. Trim (SH#1485-02)—Summer Hill Ltd.; 650/363-2600. Blinds and valance fabrication—Strictly Decorative. Llamp—John Rosselli International; 212/772-2137. Shade—Blanche P. Field. Slipcover fabric for back (Tuxedo Park #PS101-0)—Carleton V; 718/706-7780. For chair seats (Plaid SH#1485-02)—Summer Hill Ltd.; 650/363-2600. Trim for chair backs (Tassel #891991)—F. Shumacher & Co.; 800/523-1200. Welt for chairs (Miami)—Norbar Fabrics; 800/645-8501. Wall finish—Philip Parsons, Parsons Decorative Arts; 617/884-0912.

Pages 74-75 (kitchen): Decorative painting on cabinet doors and floor—Philip Parsons, Parsons Decorative Arts. Rug—Johanna Erickson; 617/926-1737. Wallpaper (Spatterware #12112-06)—Brunschwig & Fils; 212/838-7878. Jane Churchill fabric for valance (Porcelain Garden #JT03F-05) For cushions (JT14F-16)—Cowtan & Tout; 212/753-4488. Trim for valance and cushions (Circo)—Norbar Fabric; 800/645-8501. Window treatment fabrication—Strictly Decorative. Chandelier and table—Spivackís. Lantern—John Rosselli; 212/772-2137.

188

Pages 76-77 (living room): Fabric for chair and sofa pillows (Raffia #OWW-RRF1010001)—Old World Weavers; 212/355-7186. Pillow fabrication—Drape-It, Inc. Lamp shades—Blanche P. Field. Mirror—Forager House, 20 Centre St., Nantucket, MA 02554; 508/228-5977. Box—Marcoz Antiques. Rug—Stark Carpet; 212/752-9000. Fabric for armchair (New Mullion Twill)—Brunschwig & Fils; 212/838-7878. Upholstery for arm chair—Connors Design Ltd.; 508/429-4980. Flounce, duvet cover, slipcover fabric for chaise longue and club chair—F. Shumacher & Co.; 800/523-1200. Fabric for chair pillows (New MullionTwill) and fabric for trim (Nid d'Abeilles #90016-05/200)—Brunschwig & Fils; 212/838-7878. Pillows, flounce, duvet cover, slipcover for chaise longue, and club chair fabrication—Dilys Sharpe 603/744-5188. Bed pillows—Anichini; 212/679-9540. Quilt—Rockport Quilt Shoppe. Rug—Stark Carpet; 212/752-9000. Table lamp by bed—John Boone, Inc.; 212/758-0012. Lampshades—Blanche P. Field. Side table by chair—Marcoz Antiques. (Bathroom, lower right photo:) Sink—Billie Brenner, Ltd.; 617/348-2858. Wallpaper (Secret Garden #W-842-01)—Osborne & Little; 212/751-3333.

Pages 78-79 (bedroom): Wallpaper (New Lyme Park #7030-03)—Clarence House; 212/752-2890. Daybed, trundle bed, and trundle—Chester Sleep Products; 617/666-4800. Upholstery for daybed end panels—Connors Design Ltd.; 508/429-4980. Quilts—Rockport Quilt Shoppe. Fabric for flounce, pillows, and comforter (Zest Wide Stripe), fabric for duvet cover (Snappy Narrow Stripe), fabric contrast band (Savoy)—Norbar Fabrics Co.; 800/645-8501. Fabric for duvet cover—Ralph Lauren; 212/642-8700. Fabrication—Dilys Morris. Fabric for draperies (Tazwell)—Skyline Mills; 800/638-8974. Fabrication—Strictly Decorative.

Pages 80-81 (dining room): Delft plates, vase, bowl—Jason Hackler at New Hampshire Antiques Co-op. Fabric for seats—Cowtan & Tout; 212/753-4488. Chandelier—Nesle, Inc.; 212/755-0515.

Page 83 Antique garden urn—Weeds, 14 Centre St., Nantucket, MA 02554; 508/228-5200.

Pages 84-85 (kitchen and family room): Painted floor: Philip Parsons, Parsons Decorative Arts. Family room: Majolica plates—Marcoz Antiques. Coffee table—Spivack's Antiques. Jane Churchill fabric for sofa (Kempton Stripe #JT11F-14)—Cowtan & Tout; 212/753-4488. Fabric for lounge chair and welt for sofa (Valentine #4352/44)—Manuel Canovas; 212/752-9588. Fabric for armchair and sofa pillow (Clipper Ships #79683.04)—Brunschwig & Fils; 212/838-7878. Fabric welt for armchair (Circa)—Norbar Fabrics Co.; 800/645-8501. Slipcover for lounge and arm chair fabrication—Dilys Morris. Rug—Stark Carpet; 212/752-9000; Antique dealers—Spivack's Antiques; 781/235-1700l; Marcoz Antiques; 617/262-0780; Jason Hackler at New Hampshire Antiques Co-op; 603/673-8499; Quilt dealer:—Rockport Quilt Shoppe; 978/546-1001; Light fixtures—Blanche P. Field; 617/423-0715; Decorative finishes—Philip Parsons, Parsons Decorative Arts; 617/884-0912; Fabrication—Drape-It, Inc.; 617/926-8864; Strictly Decorative; 978/683-7760; Fabrication Dilys Sharpe; 603/744-5188.

INDULGENT COMFORT
PAGE 88
Interior design—Thomas Bartlett, Thomas Bartlett Interiors, 2151 Main St., Napa, CA 94559; 707/259-1234.

Pages 90-91 (living room): Thomas Bartlett armoire—Rossi Antiques; 415/671-1144. Floor lamp—Execulamp; 707/769-0990. Table lamp—La Bella Copia; 415/255-0452. Large jars—de Benedictis; 415/431-9383. Ottoman (St. Nicolas), sofas (Bella)—Sloan Miyasato; 415/431-1465. Fabric for ottoman (Antique Velvet Stripe #5153-4)—Rose Cummings; 212/758-0844. Fabric for sofas (Damasco Cellini #33705/5)—Clarence House; 212/752-2890. Bullion for sofas (Leighton chenille)—F. Shumacher & Co.; 800/523-

1200. Upholstery for ottoman—Belmar Company. Fabric for sofa pillows (Carleton #8416)—Henry Calvin Fabrics; 541/732-1996. Fringe—Decorators Walk; 713/629-6340. Tapestry pillows—Shears & Window; 415/621-0911. Fabric for armchair (Apiary Stripe)—Lee Jofa; 212/688-0444. Chinese rug—Alexander's; 415/490-5654. Fabric for draperies (Victorian Cartouche #164322)—F. Shumacher & Co.; 800/523-1200. Trim (Fair Isle Stripe Vintage)—Waverly; 800/423-5881. Fabrication—Kathleen Johnson Fine Sewing. Floral arrangement—Hedgerow, 707/253-1545.

Page 92 (sitting room): Table lamps (Plum Blossom)—International Art Properties; 415/863-3406. Lampshades—La Bella Copia (415/255-0452). Roll-arm sofa redesign—Thomas Bartlett Interiors. Fabric for roll-arm sofa (Vorban-Pervenche 8119 #5); fabric for table skirt (Perruche #2224)—Pierre Frey; 212/213-3099. Tassle trim for table skirt (CNF/2309)—Clarence House; 212/752-2890. Bullion fringe for sofa (36061/c. 9622), cording (31199/c.9622)—Houles USA; 310/652-6171. Grey Watkins fabric for Chippendale armchair (Hand-Velluto Faucigny #1410-03)—Randolph & Hein, Inc.; 415/864-3371. Antique Chinese rug—Soraya Rugs; 415/626-5757. Paintings by Massimo Pantani—Thomas Bartlett Interiors. Fabric for draperies (Victorian Cartouche 164322)—F. Shumacher & Co; 800/523-1200. Fabric trim for draperies (Fair Isle Stripe Vintage)—Waverly; 800/423-5881. Fabrication: Kathleen Johnson Fine Sewing. Cove molding design—Thomas Bartlett. Cove molding decorative painting—Carole Lansdowne; 415/824-9553.

Page 93 (table vignette): Antique English table—Evans & Gerst; 310/657-0112. Painting—View at Escazs, Costa Rica by Robert Maione—John Pence Gallery; 415/441-1138.

Pages 94-97 (dining room): Jars and bowl on Sheraton sideboard—International Art Properties; 415/863-3406. Key tassel—Houle USA; 310/652-6171. Neapolitan dining table (431)—Wroolie & Co.; 415/863-8815. Fabric for chair seats (Villers #F137120001)—Old World Weavers; 212/355-7186. Mirror—Robert Hering & Associates; 415/863-4144. Chinese rug—Alexanderís; 415/490-5654. Stone fireplace surround—Napa Valley Cast Stone; 707/258-3340. Firescreen—O Kell's Fireplace; 415/626-1110. Engravings by Pierre-Joseph Redoste; painting—W. Graham Arader Gallery; 415/788-5115. Antique floor lamp (#SL06)—McRae-Hinckley; 415/626-2726. Chair and ottoman (Mondi)—Sloan Miyasato; 415/431-1465. Fabric for chair and ottoman (Glenburne #1820-02)—Fonthill 212/755-6700). Upholstery—Belmar Company. Floral arrangement—Hedgerow; 707/253-1545. Antique English oval painting, table settings—Thomas Bartlett Interiors. Drapery fabrics (Victorian Cartouche 164322)—F. Shumacher & Co; 800/523-1200. Fabric trim for draperies (Fair Isle Stripe Vintage)— Waverly; 800/423-5881. Fabrication: Kathleen Johnson Fine Sewing. Cove molding design—Thomas Bartlett. Cove molding decorative painting—Carole Lansdown; 415/824-9553.

Pages 98-99 (indoor porch): Victorian dining chairs decorative painting—Tina Wainwright; 707/887-9733. Fabric for chairs (Guorando #4448)—Donghia 212/935-3713. Fossil stone floor—Solnhofen Natural Stone; 415/647-3088. Antique tole tray—Robert Hering & Associates; 415/863-4144. Dining table (MA-1A), chairs (ZA-289), bamboo side tables (429), and sofa (Zambales Peel)—McGuire Furniture Co.; 415/986-0812. Fabric for sofa and chair cushions (Mille Fleur #970089-15)—Lee Jofa; 212/688-0444. Brass floor lamp—Execulamp; 707/769-0990. (Bureau vignette, lower right photo)—Antique English bureau—Evans & Gerst; 310/657-0112. Sheraton chair—Challiss House; 415/397-6999. Antique tapestry pillow—Robert Hering & Associates; 415/863-4144.

Pages 100-101 (bedroom): Table lamps—International Art Properties; 415/863-3406. Lamp shades—La Bella Copia; 415/255-0452. Fabric for table skirt (Losanges Stripe #970026-1510)—Lee Jofa; 212/688-0444. Bed and headboard—Sloan Miyasato; 415/431-1465. Upholstery for headboard—Belmar Company. Fabric for bed's valance, canopy, headboard, pillows, duvet cover, skirt, and window treatment (Queen Annes Lace #167412); fabric for canopy, head board, and pillows (Ovedskloster Stripe #120070)—F Shumacher & Co.; 800/523-1200. Wall covering (Lansdowne Stripe #230/01)—Osborne & Little; 212/751-3333. Wool carpet—Thomas Bartlett Interiors. Drapery and bedding fabrication—Kathleen Johnson Fine Sewing. (Child's bedroom:) Antique desk chairs—Evans & Gerst; 310/657-0112. Antique desk lamp—La Bella Copia; 415/255-0452. Antique bed refinishing—Rossi Antiques; 415/671-1144.Tassels on chairs (#304393); tassels on slipper chair (304503); fabric for bed skirt, pillows, and table skirt (Menton Check #58422)—F. Shumacher & Co.; 800/523-1200. Fabric for slipper chair(Leicester Check #33201/A)—Clarence House; 212/752-2890. Fabric for chair seat (Astor Stripe #F1302-07); fabric for duvet cover (Musical Monkeys #10628-03)—Cowtan & Tout; 212/753-4488. Trim for window treatment (V161-043)—Scalamandre; 212/980-3888. Cabinet mural painting—Carole Lansdowne; 415/824-9553. Painting Monkey in Costume by Carlo Marchiari—Ca-toga Galleria-Arte; 707/942-3900.

Pages 102-103 (dining room): Wall covering (damask)—Scalamandré 212/980-3888. Banquette—Thomas Bartlett Interiors. Fabric for banquette and pillows (Florence Texture #190776)—Brunschwig & Fils; 212/838-7878. Fabric for pillows (linen velvet #N-149-11)—Kneedler Fauchere; 415/861-1011. Erika Brunson tables—Randolph & Hein (415/864-3371). Antique dining table, buffet, crystal chandelier, and chairs—Antonio's; 415/ 781-1737. Fabric for cushions (linen velvet #4702)—Henry Calvin Fabrics; 541/732-1996. Cording (Yves Compote); tassels for cushions (Mitzi Compote)—Robert Allen 800/333-3776. Upholstery for chair cushions—Belmar Company. Rug (Villandry)—Stark Carpet; 212/752-9000.

Page 104 (bedroom): Wall covering—Hinson & Co.; 212/688-5538. Fabric for vanity (Glynnis #HCF32313-30) and throw—McRae Hinckley; 415/626-2726. Fabric for bed pillows and duvet cover (Chelsea Gardens #1299-01)—Summer Hill; 650/363-2600. Louis XVI-style stool—John Lagvy Co.; 415/647-6433. Table skirt, stool, and window treatment (Coroux glazed chintz)—Brunschwig & Fils; 212/838-7878. Vanity table—Bartlett Interiors.

Page 105 (sitting room): Antique corner cabinet—Antonio's; 415/781-1737. Fabric for table skirt (Bellini Stripe)—Cowtan & Tout; 212/753-4488. Fabric for draperies (silk taffeta #32705-25 and #32705-5)—Clarence House; 212/752-2890. Palmer Designs drapery rods and rings; Nesle, Inc. crystal chandelier (#MFR-8); Ed Hardy Louis XVI-style chair—Shears & Window; 415/621-0911. Empire-style tea table (#TT-504)—J. Robert Scott; 310/659-4910. Fabric for chairs and ottoman (Francesca #98333-18 and #98333-1)—Scalamandré; 212/980-3888. Drapery fabrication—Kathleen Johnson Fine Sewing. Carpet—Thomas Bartlett Interiors. (Bathroom:) Phylrich lavatory set—The Bath & Beyond; 415/552-5001. Vanity cabinet; glass chandelier (Murano) Thomas Bartlett Interiors. Palmer Hargrave wall sconces (Baton)—Kneedler Fauchere; 415/861-1011. Sconce shades—LaBella Copia; 415/255-0452. Wallcovering (Lansdowne Stripe #VW1230/01)—Osborne & Little; 212/751-3333. Half-moon mirror—Randolph & Hein; 425/864-3371. Cachepots—Drum & Co. (415/551-1538). Antique Chinese rug—Alexander's (415/490-5654).

Pages 106-107 (living room): Antique footstool, column, and armchairs—Antonioís; 415/ 781-1737. Fabric for armchairs (Satin Stripe #1236M-011)—Scalamandre; 212/980-3888. Fabric for sofa (Juliana damask #7450)—Henry Calvin Fabrics; 541/732-1996. Pillows—Claire Thompson; 415/986-4453. Leather for antique bench—S. H. Frank; 415/551-1405. Antique Chinese planter behind sofa—Drum & Co.; 415/551-1538. Fabric for draperies (Silk Stripe #C2-201-

10)—Christopher Norman; 212/644-4100. Trim (#57752)—F. Shumacher & Co.; 800/523-1200. Fabrication—Kathleen Johnson Fine Sewing. Needlepoint rug—Stark Carpet; 212/752-9000. Garden seats: Evans & Gerst; 310/657-0112.

Page 108 (planter vignette): Stone wall faux painting through Thomas Bartlett Interiors. Furnishings and custom designs—Thomas Bartlett Interiors, 707/259-1234; Antique dealer—Antonio's, 701 Bryant St., San Francisco, CA 94107; 415/781-1737; Decorative painting artists—Tina Wainwright; 707/887-9733; Carole Lansdowne; 415/824-9553; Paul Akimoff through Thomas Bartlett Interiors; Upholstery—Belmar Company; 415/621-7447; Window treatments, pillows, and bedding fabrication—Kathleen Johnson Fine Sewing; 707/942-9442.

PRETTY AND POLISHED
PAGE 110

Interior design—Paula Perlini, Paula Perlini, Inc., 165 E. 35th St., New York, NY; 212/889-6551.

Page 113 (dining room): Fabric for draperies (wool gabardine); festoon window treatment (sheer wool challis); loveseat (velvet); and wall covering—Clarence House; 212/752-2890. Fabric for Queen Ann dining chairs (Tapestry)—Brunschwig & Fils; 212/838-7878.

Pages 114-115 (living room): Paint for walls (Oriental Silk)—Benjamin Moore, 800/826-2623. Rug—Stark Carpet; 212/752-9000. Fabric for sofa (cotton damask)—Scalamandré; 212/980-3888. Fabric for sofa pillows—Old World Weavers; 212/355-7186. Fabric for club chairs (damask)—Roger Arlington; 212/752-5288. Fabric for draperies—Clarence House; 212/752-2890. Fabric for festoon (Sheer Voile)—Hinson; 212/688-5538.

Page 116 (library): Fabric for chair (Tapestry)—Brunschwig & Fils; 212/838-7878. For seat—Clarence House; 212/752-2890. For draperies (Passion Flower)—Rose Cummings; 212/758-0844.

Page 117 (library combination dining room): Fabric for draperies (Glen Plaid) and fabric on chairs—Clarence House; 212/752-2890.

Pages 118-119 (living room): Paint for walls (Apricot Glaze)—Benjamin Moore; 800/826-2623. Sisal rug (Sultanbad custom design)—Stark Carpet; 212/752-9000. Fabric for Louis VI loveseat, Louis IV chairs, ottoman, pillow, and draperies—Clarence House; 212/838-2890. Fabric for sofa—F. Schumacher & Co; 800/332-3384.

Page 121 (living room): Fabric for sofa (damask)—Schumacher; 800/332-3384. Fabric for Louis IV chair and sofa pillows—Clarence House; 212/752-2890. Bedroom, lower left photo: Wallpaper—Clarence House (212/752-2890). (Hall, lower right photo): Fabric for French chair (cotton)—Fortuny; 212/753-7153. Antiques and accessories—Paula Perlini, Inc.; 212/889-6551.

CONFIDENCE WITH COLOR
PAGE 134

Interior design—Kelly Gale Amen, ASID, Kelly Gale Amen Design, P.O. Box 66447, Houston, TX 77266; 713/522-1410.; fax: 713/521-1647; e-mail: kelly@kga.net.; Website: http://www.kga.net.

Pages 136-137 (dining room): Console and wall border painting—Nancy Ruby; 713/523-6230. Fabric for draperies—Walter Lee Culp & Associates; 713/623-4670. Fabric for cushions—Brunschwig & Fils; 212/838-7878.

Page 138 (foyer): Fabric for antique bench—Scalamandré; 212/980-3888. Painting by Kermit Oliver—Hooks Gallery; 713/522-0718.

Pages 140-141 (living room): Paintings by Robert Rector—Macon & Co.; 404/582-0044. Antique Persian rug—Denton Jones Showroom 713/961-1183. Fabric for roll-arm chair—Beacon Hill; 800/921-5050. Fabric for ottoman body (Broadway Cordon Quartz); fabric for ottoman skirt and trim (Empire Stripe)—Randolpf & Hein; 415/864-3371. Floral arrangement—David Brown Florist.

Pages 142-143 (living room): Stone-topped bronze bench— KGA Metal. Fabric for sofa—Brunschwig & Fils; 212/838-7878. Fabric for draperies—F. Schumacher & Co.; 800/332-3384. Finish on walls—Theo Ostler. Music room: Painting Orange Works on Paper by Michael Tracy—Macon & Co.; 404/582-0044. Fabric for armchair—Beacon Hill; 800/921-5050. Landing: Sculpture by Chris Moulder—Macon & Co.; 404/582-0044.

Page 144 (entry): Aluminum console—KGA Metal.

Page 145 (bedroom): Bed—KGA. Bed linens—Pratesi 713/840-8882. Chair and ottoman—Roche-Bobois USA (800/972-8375). Floral arrangement—David Brown Florist.

Pages 146-147 (family room): Antique Chinese rug—Denton Jones Showroom (713/961-1183). Round painting In Earth ë Diurnal Course by Vanita Smithey—M D Modern; 713/526-5966. Floor lamp—Roche-Bobois USA; 800/972-8375. Bench in front of fireplace—Beacon Hill; 800/921-5050. Imported Venetian glass mirror and coffee table—Decorators Walk; 713/629-6340. Fabric for sofa and club chair (Broadway Cordon Quartz); fabric for skirt and trim (Empire Stripe)—Randolph & Hein; 415/864-3371. Painted details on sofa—Barbara Jones; 713/522-1414.. Pillows and cat bed—KGA. Cast aluminum armchair—KGA Metal. Faux finish on walls—Theo Ostler Floral arrangement—David Brown Florist; KGA/furniture and accessories—Dorian Bahr Muti-line Showroom; 214/698-9936; KGA Metal/ metal furniture—Macon & Co.; 404/582-0044; Nancy Littlejohn Fine Art; 713/229-0222; Decorative painters—Theo Ostler; 713/524-7611; Nancy Ruby; 713/523-6230; Barbara Jones 713/522-1414; Floral arrangements—David Brown Florist; 713/861-4048.

CULTURAL CROSSROADS
PAGE 150

Interior design—Doug Rasar Interior Design, 9400 Vineyard Crest, Bellevue, WA 98004; 425/450-9911; fax: 425/450-1199.

Architect—Brandt Hollinger, AIA, Hollinger Architects, 603 Stewart St., #519, Seattle, WA 98101; 206/624-6855.

Pages 152-153 (dining room): Antique English breakfront—Jean Williams Antiques, 115 S. Jackson St., Seattle, WA 98101; 206/622-1110. Switzer lantern light fixture—Wayne Martin, Inc.; 503/221-1555. Jardinere on console—Bergdorf Goodman; 212/753-7300. Chippendale-style chairs—Doug Rasar Interior Design.

Pages 154-155 (sunroom): Switzer lantern light fixture; Palmer Hargrave sconces—Wayne Martin, Inc.; 503/221-1555. Nancy Corzine sofa —Elinor & Verve, Inc.; 206/447-9250. Fabric for sofa and pillows (floral)—Brunschwig & Fils; 212/838-7878. Ottoman base—MacKenzie-Childs Ltd.; 212/570-6050. Fabric for ottoman, sofa pillows (check); fabric for club chairs—Clarence House; 212/752-2890. Fabric for draperies—Cowtan & Tout; 212/753-4488. Fauteuil chair and drapery rods—Doug Rasar.

Pages 156-157 (living room/library): Antique candlesticks—Porter Davis Antiques, 103 University St., Seattle, WA 98101; 206/622-5310. French side table—Waldo; 212/308-8688. Lamp on side table—John Rosselli International; 212/772-2137. Fabric for roll-arm chairs (check)—Clarence House; 212/752-2890. Fabric for sofa—Brunschwig & Fils; 212/838-7878. Sofa and coffee table—Doug Rasar Design.

Page 159 (entry): Silk shade on ceiling light fixture—Fortuny; 212/753-7153. Geometric stenciled motif design on wood floor—Doug Rasar Interior Design.

Pages 160-161 (library): Mandarin Rose porcelain—Bergdorf Goodman; 212/753-7300. Antique partners desk—Sentimento (212/750-3111). (Living room): Fabric for armchair (Needle-nose carpet)—Pande Cameron & Co.; 212/686-8330. Antique French sconce and reproduction mirror—John Rosselli International; 212/772-2137. Fabric for sofa (silk): Brunschwig & Fils (212/838-7878). Pillows (Aubusson Tapestry)—Sentimento; 212/750-3111.

Page 162 (French-style chair vignette): Fabric for French-

style armchair (silk)—Brunschwig & Fils; 212/838-7878.

Page 163 (bedroom): Side table and lamp—John Rosselli International 212/772-2137). Bed linens—Takashimaya; 800/753-2038. Engravings over bed—Doug Rasar.

Pages 164-165 (dining room): Fabric on cornice (Arts and Crafts-style)—Clarence House; 212/752-2890. Fabric between coffered beams (silk); fabric for chair by window (striped)—Scalamandré; 212/980-3888. Fireplace surround tiles—Pratt & Larson Tile; 503/231-9464. Table linens—Table Top Shop, 206/526-8480.

Pages 166-167 (living room): Sofas and glass coffee table—Doug Rasar Interior Design. Dining room—Antique table: Epel & Lacroze Antiques, Inc.; 212/355-0050; Custom furniture and accessories—Doug Rasar, Doug Rasar Interior Design; 425/450-9911.

ACHIEVING TIMELESS EASE
PAGE 170

Interior design—Alessandra Branca, Branca Inc.,1325 N. State Pkwy, Chicago, ILL 60610; 312/787-6123.

Pages 172-174 (living room): Antique Louis XIV armchair and candlestick sconce—Sotheby's; 212/606-7000. Fabric for Louis XIV armchair, sofa, pillow, and draperies (striped)—Cowtan & Tout; 212/753-4488. Slipcover fabric for sofa—Scalamandré; 212/980-3888. Fabric for table skirt—Christopher Norman; 212/644-4100. Fabric for Louis XV chair in front of window—Manuel Canovas; 212/752-9588. Fabric for chair pillow—Christopher Norman; 212/644-4100. Sisal—Stark Carpet 212/752-9000. Club chairs; Rubelli fabric for club chairs; hand-painted pillow on chair by Anna Chiara Branca; sofa; pillows; glaze on walls—Branca, Inc.

Pages 176-179 (dining room): Fabric for Italian armchair seats—Cowtan & Tout; 212/753-4488. Fabric for chair cushions (velvet)—Clarence House; 212/752-2890. Antique wall sconce—Sotheby's; 212/606-7000. Vienna crystal—Baccarat; 800/845-1928. Fabric for top layer of table—Lee Jofa; 212/688-0444. Fabric trim for tablecloth—Brunschwig & Fils; 212/838-7878. Fabric for table skirt—Christopher Norman; 212/644-4100. Paintings by sconce and fireplace screen by Anna Chiara Branca.

Pages 180-181 (bedroom): Wallpaper—Clarence House; 212/752-2890. Fabric for bed draperies—Brunschwig & Fils; 212/838-7878. Duvet cover and pillows—Pratesi Linens; 713/840-8882. Headboard; lamp, chair, and ottoman—Branca. Fabric for chair and ottoman—Manuel Canovas (212/752-9588); fabric for pillow—Cowtan & Tout; 212/753-4488. Rug—Stark Carpets (212/752-9000).

Pages 182-183 (family room): Chair at desk—Minton-Spindel; 310.836-0403. Fabric for chair—F. Shumacher & Co.; 800/332-3384. For table skirt—Waverly; 800/423-5881. Wing chairs—Branca. Fabric for chairs—Clarence House; 212/752-2890. Carpet—Stark Carpet (212/752-9000).

Page 184 (family room): Painting over sofa—John Rosselli; 212/772-2137. Sofa; metal side table; sleigh-back chairs; fabric for sofa, fabric for sleigh-back chair backs, fabric for cupboard treatments (Carlton)—Branca, Inc. Fabric for sleigh-back chair fronts and sofa pillows—Clarence House; 212/752-2890. Breakfast area—Stone-based table—Stone Yard; 312/661-1900. Paintings by Redoute, Jensen Ironworks chandelier, Cherubini teapot, metal side table, ottoman, fabric for bench (Carlton); rug (Ori); Directoire-style chairs—Branca Inc. Fabric for ottoman—Payne Fabrics; 800/543-4322. Fabric for Directoire-style chair seats—Branca Clarence House; 212/752-2890.

Page 185 (family room): Braquenie & Valentino fabric for Directoire armchairs; Steve Mittman club chairs; Braquenie fabric for chairs; Jensen Louis XVI-style desk.

Page 186 (bedroom): Wallpaper—Clarence House; 212/752-2890. Carpet—Stark Carpet; 212/752-9000. Lamp and CD holder—Pottery Barn 800/922-5507. Furniture, artwork, and accessories—Alessandra Branca, Branca Inc.; 312/787-6123.

INDEX